Catherine Bouquerel

Knitting for Teddies

Photography by Alain Cornu

TRAFALGAR SQUARE PUBLISHING

To Michaël, Matthieu, Hugo, Yeni, Lola, Maëva, Laura, Léo, Bettina, Maëlyn.
To all the babies still to come.

First published in the United States of America in 2003 by
Trafalgar Square Publishing, North Pomfret, VT 05053

Printed in Spain by Bookprint, S.L., Barcelona

ISBN 1 57076240 6

Library of Congress Catalog Card Number: 2002111998

Contents

Mother Bear and Baby Bear are now watching the dragonflies fluttering about in the warm evening sun. They have been weeding the flower beds and watering the plants, and they have picked a bunch of flowers to give to Father Bear when he gets home after work. Chrysanthemums are growing in pots standing near the back door of their house.

Mother Bear

To fit a bear 13½in (34cm) tall

Wool
Robin Columbine 4-ply (machine washable): 1 ball each of Regal (6822) and Cream (6801); bright red, rose pink and green embroidery cotton

Needles
1 pair no. 2 (3mm), 1 pair no. 3 (3¼mm) and an embroidery needle

Materials
1 strip of Velcro, 4in (10cm) long

Stitches
Garter stitch: knit every row
Stockinette (stocking) stitch (st st): knit 1 row, purl 1 row
Swiss darning: on the finished sweater cover individual knitted stitches with V-shaped stitches worked in embroidery cotton

Gauge (Tension)
Using no. 3 (3¼mm) needles and measured over stockinette (stocking) stitch, 31 stitches and 44 rows measure 4in (10cm) square.

Baby Bear

To fit a bear 9½in (24cm) tall

Wool
Robin Columbine 4-ply (machine washable): 1 ball each of Regal (6822) and Cream (6801); bright red, rose pink and green embroidery cotton

Needles
1 pair no. 2 (3mm), 1 pair no. 3 (3¼mm) and an embroidery needle

Materials
2 snaps (press-studs)

Stitches
Garter stitch: knit every row
Stockinette (stocking) stitch (st st): knit 1 row, purl 1 row
Fair Isle (Jacquard): follow Chart B, using the stranding method (carrying the yarn not in use at the back of the work)
Swiss darning: on the finished dress cover individual knitted stitches with V-shaped stitches worked in embroidery cotton

Gauge (Tension)
Using no. 3 (3¼mm) needles and measured over stockinette (stocking) stitch, 31 stitches and 44 rows measure 4in (10cm) square.

Child

To fit a child 3/6 months

Wool
Robin Columbine 4-ply (machine washable): 4 balls each of Regal (6822) and Cream (6801); bright red, rose pink and green embroidery cotton

Needles
1 pair no. 2 (3mm), 1 pair no. 3 (3¼mm) and an embroidery needle

Materials
6 small buttons

Stitches
Garter stitch: knit every row
Stockinette (stocking) stitch (st st): knit 1 row, purl 1 row
Swiss darning: on the finished sweater cover individual knitted stitches with V-shaped stitches worked in embroidery cotton

Gauge (Tension)
Using no. 3 (3¼mm) needles and measured over stockinette (stocking) stitch, 31 stitches and 44 rows measure 4in (10cm) square.

Mother Bear

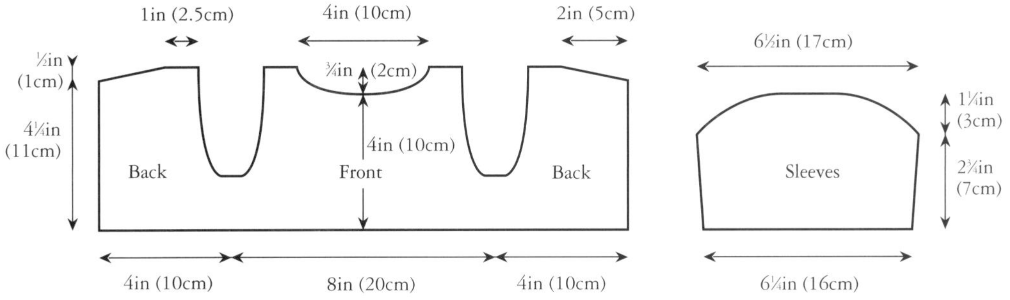
1in (2.5cm)
4in (10cm)
2in (5cm)
½in (1cm)
¾in (2cm)
4¼in (11cm)
4in (10cm)
Back
Front
Back
4in (10cm)
8in (20cm)
4in (10cm)
6½in (17cm)
1¼in (3cm)
2¾in (7cm)
Sleeves
6¼in (16cm)

Baby Bear

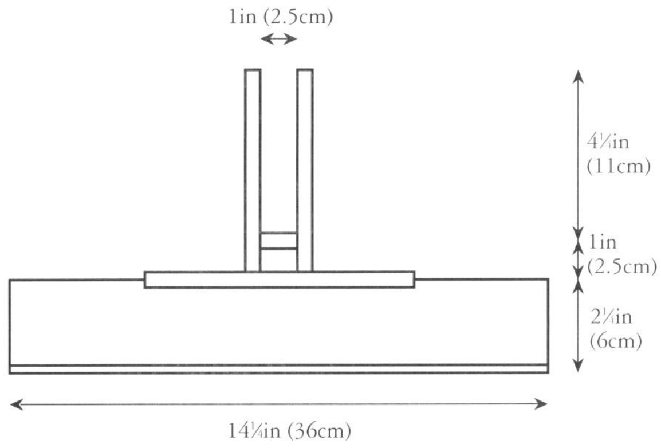
1in (2.5cm)
4¼in (11cm)
1in (2.5cm)
2¼in (6cm)
14¼in (36cm)

Child

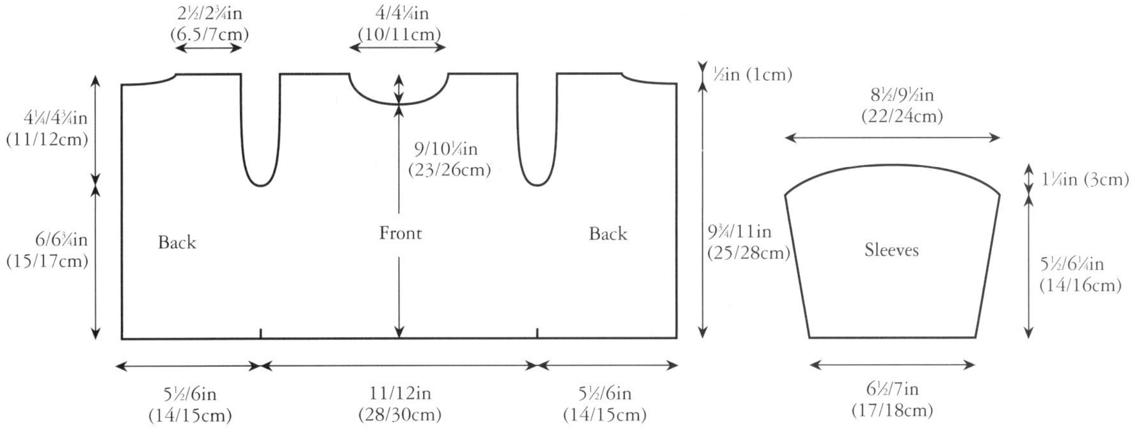
2½/2¾in (6.5/7cm)
4/4¼in (10/11cm)
½in (1cm)
4¼/4¾in (11/12cm)
9/10¼in (23/26cm)
6/6¾in (15/17cm)
Back
Front
Back
9¾/11in (25/28cm)
8½/9½in (22/24cm)
1¼in (3cm)
Sleeves
5½/6¼in (14/16cm)
5½/6in (14/15cm)
11/12in (28/30cm)
5½/6in (14/15cm)
6½/7in (17/18cm)

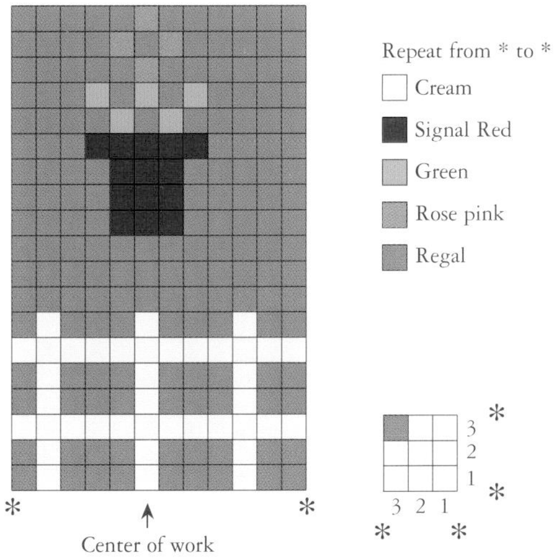
Repeat from * to *
Cream
Signal Red
Green
Rose pink
Regal
*
*
Center of work
3
2
1
3 2 1
*
*
*
*

Chart A

Chart B

Mother Bear

Front and back

The body of the sweater is worked as a single piece, beg at the bottom. Using no. 2 (3mm) needles and Regal, cast on 127 sts. Work 4 rows in garter st.

Change to no. 3 (3¼mm) needles and st st. Begin to follow Chart A, using the stranding method of Fair Isle (Jacquard).

When the work measures 1½in (4cm) from the beg, shape the armholes. Work 28 sts (left back), bind (cast) off 8 sts, knit 55 sts (across the front), bind (cast) off 8 sts, work the remaining 28 sts. Cont in st st on these 28 sts (right back), shaping the armhole by binding (casting) off on the inside edge on alt rows 2 sts once and 1 st twice (24 sts). Cont in st st until the work measures 4¼in (11cm) from the beg. Shape the neck by binding (casting) off on the outside edge on alt rows 6 sts twice and 4 sts once (8 sts). When the work measures 4¾in (12cm) from the beg, bind (cast) off the remaining 8 sts to form the shoulder.

Work the left back in the same way, reversing all shaping.

Pick up the 55 sts across the front and work in st st, shaping the armholes at both sides by binding (casting) off on alt rows 2 sts once and 1 st twice (47 sts). Cont in st st until work measures 4in (10cm) from the beg. Shape the neck by binding (casting) off the center 9 sts. Working each side separately, bind (cast) off on alt rows 3 sts twice, 2 sts twice and 1 st once (8 sts).

When the work measures 4¾in (12cm) from the beg, bind (cast) off the remaining 8 sts to form the shoulder. Repeat for the other shoulder, reversing all shaping.

Sleeves

Using no. 2 (3mm) needles and Regal, cast on 51 sts. Work 4 rows in garter st.

Change to no. 3 (3¼mm) needles and st st. Begin to follow Chart A, using the stranding method of Fair Isle (Jacquard). When the work measures 1¼in (3cm) from the beg, inc one st at each end (53 sts). Cont in st st. When the work measures 2¾in (7cm) from the beg, bind (cast) off at each end of alt rows 3 sts once, 2 sts once, 1 st once, 2 sts once and 3 sts three times. Bind (cast) off the remaining 19 sts. Work the other sleeve to match.

Collar

Using no. 2 (3mm) needles and Cream, cast on 4 sts. Work in garter st, inc 1 st on right-hand edge on alt rows five times. Work 32 rows, then dec 1 st at the right-hand edge on alt rows five times. Bind (cast) off the remaining 4 sts. Work another collar to match.

Making up

Following Chart A and using embroidery cotton, stitch the pots of flowers around the bottom of the sweater and the sleeves, positioning the bottom of the flowerpot 3 rows above the Fair Isle (Jacquard) pattern.

Stitch the shoulders together and close the arm seams. Set in and stitch the sleeves in position. Using no. 2 (3mm) needles and Regal, pick up 35 sts along one back opening. Work 4 rows in garter st. Repeat on the other back opening. Using no. 2 (3mm) needles and Regal, pick up 84 sts around the neck. Work 2 rows in st st. Bind (cast) off. Attach the collars to each side of the back opening, positioning them so that they meet at the center front. Attach the Velcro to the back opening.

Baby Bear

Using no. 2 (3mm) needles and Regal, cast on 120 sts. Work 6 rows in garter st.

Change to no. 3 (3¼mm) needles and st st. Begin to follow Chart B, using the stranding method of Fair Isle (Jacquard). When the work measures 2¼in (6cm) from the beg and working on a purl row, K2tog across the row (60 sts).

Using no. 2 (3mm) needles and Regal, work ½in (1cm) in K1, P1 rib. Bind (cast) off 21 sts at each end (18 sts). Make the pinafore front. Work in K1, P1 rib for 5 sts, work in st st over the center 8 sts and end with K1, P1 rib. Cont to work in pattern for 1in (2.5cm), then work 4 rows in garter st over the center 8 sts, but cont to work in rib at the sides. Bind (cast) off the center sts. Working on each side separately, cont in K1, P1 rib until each strap measures 4¼in (11cm). Bind (cast) off.

Embroider a pot of flowers (see Chart A) on the pinafore front. Stitch a snap (press-stud) at the end of each strap, positioning the other part of each stud at the center back of the skirt. Use Regal to plait or crochet two cords. Attach these to the center back and fasten them with a bow.

Child

Front and back

The body of the sweater is worked as a single piece, beg at the bottom. Using no. 2 (3mm) needles and Regal, cast on 173/185 sts. Work 4 rows in garter st.

Change to no. 3 (3¼mm) needles and st st. Begin to follow Chart A, using the stranding method of Fair Isle (Jacquard). When the work measures 6/6¾in (15/17cm) from the beg, shape the armholes. Work 39/42 sts (left back), bind (cast) off 8 sts, knit 79/85 sts (across the front), bind (cast) off 8 sts, work the remaining 39/42 sts. Cont in st st on these 39/42 sts (right back), shaping the armhole by binding (casting) off on the inside edge on alt rows 2 sts once and 1 st twice (35/38 sts). Cont in st st until the work measures 9¾/11in (25/28cm) from the beg. Shape the neck by binding (casting) off on the outside edge on alt rows 8/10 sts once and 7/7 sts once (20/21 sts). When the work measures 10¼/11½in (26/29cm) from the beg, bind (cast) off the remaining 20/21 sts to form the shoulder.

Work the left back in the same way, reversing all shaping.

Pick up the 79/85 sts across the front and work in st st, shaping the armholes at both sides by binding (casting) off on alt rows 2 sts once and 1 st twice (71/77 sts). Cont in st st until the work measures 9/10¼in (23/26cm) from the beg. Shape the neck by binding (casting) off the center 9/13 sts. Working each side separately, bind (cast) off on alt rows 3 sts twice, 2 sts twice and 1 st once (20/21 sts). When the work measures 10¼/11½in (26/29cm) from the beg, bind (cast) off the remaining 20/21 sts to form the shoulder. Repeat for the other shoulder, reversing all shaping.

Sleeves

Using no. 2 (3mm) needles and Regal, cast on 53/57 sts. Work 4 rows in garter st.

Change to no. 3 (3¼mm) needles and st st. Begin to follow Chart A, using the stranding method of Fair Isle (Jacquard). Inc 1 st at each end of every sixth row 8/9 times (69/75 sts). Cont in st st. When the work measures 5½/6¼in (14/16cm) from the beg, bind (cast) off at each end of alt rows 3 sts once, 2 sts once, 1 st once, 2 sts once and 3 sts three times. Bind (cast) off the remaining 35/41 sts. Work the other sleeve to match.

Collar

Using no. 2 (3mm) needles and Cream, cast on 4 sts. Work in garter st, inc 1 st on right-hand edge on alt rows five times. Work 40/46 rows, then dec 1 st at the right-hand edge on alt rows five times. Bind (cast) off the remaining 4 sts. Work another collar to match.

Making up

Following Chart A and using embroidery cotton, stitch the pots of flowers around the bottom of the sweater and the sleeves, positioning the bottom of the flowerpot 3 rows above the Fair Isle (Jacquard) pattern.

Stitch the shoulders together and close the arm seams. Set in and stitch the sleeves in position.

Using no. 2 (3mm) needles and Regal, pick up 72/81 sts along one back opening. Work 4 rows in garter st. Repeat on the other back opening, but working 6 small buttonholes, the first 3 sts from the top, the remaining 12/14 sts apart. Position the buttons on the other buttonband to match.

Using no. 2 (3mm) needles and Regal, pick up 92/98 sts around the neck. Work 2 rows in st st. Bind (cast) off. Attach the collars to each side of the back opening, positioning them so that they meet at the center front.

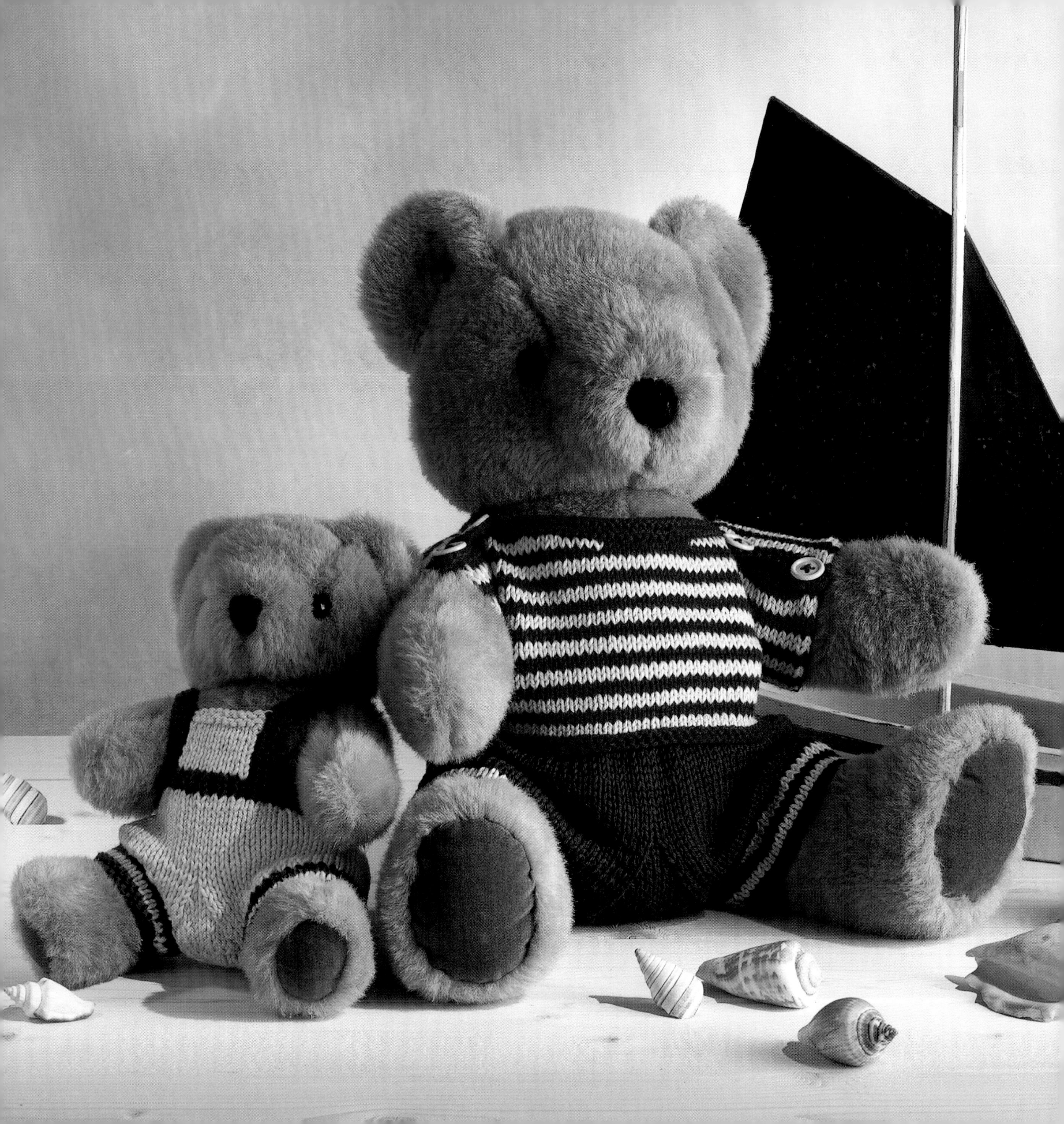

Mother Bear and Baby Bear have been sailing in their yacht, and now they are collecting seashells from the beach. When Baby Bear puts one of the shells to his ear, he can hear the sound of the sea. They are waiting to see the sun setting over the horizon, and in the meantime they are watching seagulls wheeling about over the waves.

At the Seaside

Mother Bear

To fit a bear 13½in (34cm) tall

Wool
Wendy Supreme Luxury Cotton 4-ply (machine washable): 1 ball of Rich Navy (1829), Ivory (1834) and Red Wine (1835)

Needles
1 pair no. 2 (3mm) and 2 pairs no. 3 (3¼mm)

Materials
Dark blue elastic
4 cream-colored buttons, each ¾in (15mm) across

Stitches
Garter stitch: knit every row
Rib: K2, P2
Striped stockinette (stocking) stitch (st st): 2 rows Ivory, 2 rows Red Wine
Simple decrease: on a knit row decrease 1 st by slipping the next st purlwise onto the right-hand needle, knit the next st, then pass the slipped st over the knitted st and off the needle (sl1, K1, psso).

Gauge (Tension)
Using no. 3 (3¼mm) needles and measured over stockinette (stocking) stitch, 29 stitches and 36 rows measure 4in (10cm) square.

Baby Bear

To fit a bear 9½in (24cm) tall

Wool
Wendy Supreme Luxury Cotton 4-ply (machine washable): 1 ball each of Rich Navy (1829) and Red Wine (1835)

Needles
1 pair no. 2 (3mm) and 2 pairs no. 3 (3¼mm)

Materials
2 cream-colored buttons, each ¾in (15mm) across
Buttonhole cotton

Stitches
Garter stitch: knit every row
Rib: K1, P1
Stockinette (stocking) stitch (st st): knit 1 row, purl 1 row
Simple decrease: on a knit row decrease 1 st by slipping the next st purlwise onto the right-hand needle, knit the next st, then pass the slipped st over the knitted st and off the needle (sl1, K1, psso).

Gauge (Tension)
Using no. 3 (3¼mm) needles and measured over stockinette (stocking) stitch, 29 stitches and 36 rows measure 4in (10cm) square.

Child

To fit a child 3/6 months

Wool
Wendy Supreme Luxury Cotton 4-ply (machine washable): 3/4 balls each of Rich Navy (1829), Ivory (1834) and Red Wine (1835)

Needles
1 pair no. 2 (3mm) and 2 pairs no. 3 (3¼mm)

Materials
Dark blue elastic
6 cream-colored buttons, each ¾in (15mm) across

Stitches
Garter stitch: knit every row
Rib: K2, P2
Striped stockinette (stocking) stitch (st st): 2 rows Ivory, 2 rows Red Wine
Simple decrease: on a knit row decrease 1 st by slipping the next st purlwise onto the right-hand needle, knit the next st, then pass the slipped st over the knitted st and off the needle (sl1, K1, psso).

Gauge (Tension)
Using no. 3 (3¼mm) needles and measured over stockinette (stocking) stitch, 29 stitches and 36 rows measure 4in (10cm) square.

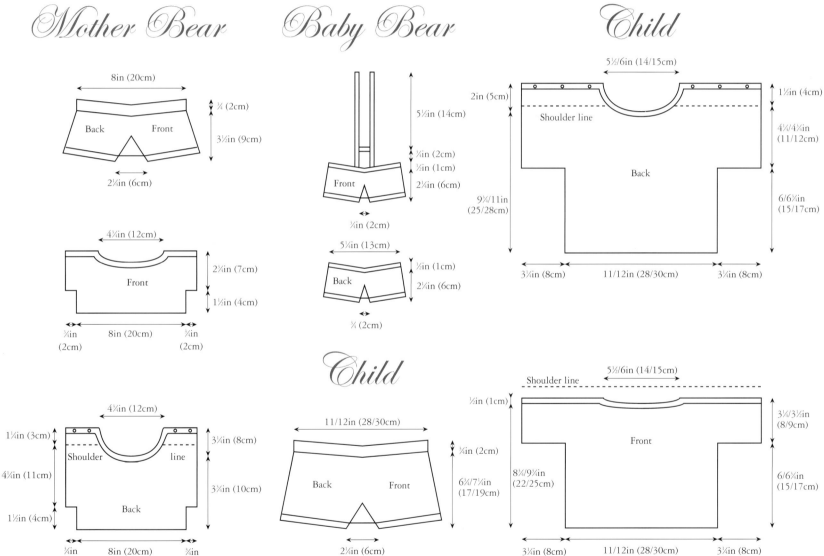

Mother Bear

8in (20cm)

¾in (2cm)

Back   Front

3½in (9cm)

2¼in (6cm)

4¾in (12cm)

2¾in (7cm)

Front

1½in (4cm)

¾in (2cm)   8in (20cm)   ¾in (2cm)

1¼in (3cm)

4¾in (12cm)

3¼in (8cm)

Shoulder   line

4¼in (11cm)

3¾in (10cm)

1½in (4cm)

Back

¾in (2cm)   8in (20cm)   ¾in (2cm)

Baby Bear

5½in (14cm)

¾in (2cm)

½in (1cm)

2¼in (6cm)

Front

¾in (2cm)

5¼in (13cm)

½in (1cm)

2¼in (6cm)

Back

¾in (2cm)

Child

11/12in (28/30cm)

⅜in (2cm)

Back   Front

6¾/7½in (17/19cm)

2¼in (6cm)

Child

5½/6in (14/15cm)

2in (5cm)

1½in (4cm)

Shoulder line

4¼/4¾in (11/12cm)

Back

9¾/11in (25/28cm)

6/6¾in (15/17cm)

3¼in (8cm)   11/12in (28/30cm)   3¼in (8cm)

Shoulder line

5½/6in (14/15cm)

½in (1cm)

3¼/3½in (8/9cm)

Front

8¾/9¾in (22/25cm)

6/6¾in (15/17cm)

3¼in (8cm)   11/12in (28/30cm)   3¼in (8cm)

Knitting for Teddies

At the Seaside

Mother Bear

Shorts

Work the back first. Using no. 2 (3mm) needles and Rich Navy, cast on 24 sts. Work 4 rows in garter st. Change to no. 3 (3¼mm) needles and work in st st, inc 1 st at each end of the next row (26 sts). Work 2 rows in Ivory, 2 rows in Rich Navy and 2 rows in Ivory. Leave the sts on a spare needle. Work the other leg to match.

Work the gusset. Using no. 3 (3¼mm) needles and Rich Navy, cast on 16 sts. Slip the stitches onto one of the needles between the sts held for the two legs. Work in st st, beg with the 16 sts in the center, picking up on each row 5 sts four times and 6 sts once from each group of leg sts. At the same time, on 8 alt rows at the right-hand gusset edge sl1, K1, psso and on the left side K2tog (52 sts). When the center of the work measures 3½in (9cm), change to no. 2 (3mm) needles and work ¾in (2cm) in K2, P2 rib. Bind (cast) off loosely. Work the front to match. Join the side seams. Sow the inner leg and gusset seams together. Stitch 2 rows of elastic to the inside of the waistband.

T-shirt front

Using no. 2 (3mm) needles and Red Wine, cast on 53 sts. Work 4 rows in garter st. Change to no. 3 (3¼mm) needles and cont in striped st st (working 2 rows in Ivory, 2 rows in Red Wine). When the work

measures 1½in (4cm) from the beg, work the sleeves, casting on 5 sts at the beg and end of the next row (63 sts). Cont in pattern until the work measures 3¼in (8cm). Put the center 11 sts on a spare needle and work the shoulders separately, binding (casting) off at the neck edge on alt rows 5 sts twice. Using no. 2 (3mm) needles and Red Wine, work 4 rows, including the sts held at the center, in garter st. Bind (cast) off loosely.

T-shirt back

Using no. 2 (3mm) needles and Red Wine, cast on 53 sts. Work 4 rows in garter st. Change to no. 3 (3¼mm) needles and cont in striped st st (working 2 rows in Ivory, 2 rows in Red Wine). When the work measures 1½in (4cm) from the beg, work the sleeves, casting on 5 sts at the beg and end of the next row (63 sts). Cont in pattern until the work measures 4in (10cm). Put the center 7 sts on a spare needle and work the shoulders separately, binding (casting) off at the neck edge on alt rows 3 sts once, 2 sts twice and 1 st five times. Using no. 2 (3mm) needles and Red Wine, work 4 rows, including the sts held at the center, in garter st. On the second row work 2 evenly spaced buttonholes on each shoulder piece. Bind (cast) off loosely.

Making up

Stitch buttons on the front shoulders to match the buttonholes. Close the side and underarm seams.

Baby Bear

Back

Using no. 2 (3mm) needles and Rich Navy, cast on 17 sts. Work 4 rows in garter st. Change to no. 3 (3¼mm) needles and cont in st st, working 2 rows in Ivory and 2 rows in Rich Navy. Leave the sts on a spare needle. Work the other leg to match.

Work the gusset. Using no. 3 (3¼mm) needles and Ivory, cast on 8 sts. Slip the stitches onto one of the needles between the sts held for the two legs. Work in st st, beg with the 16 sts in the center and picking up on each row 4 sts three times and 5 sts once from the leg sts. At the same time, on 4 alt rows at the right-hand gusset edge sl1, K1, psso and on the left side K2tog (34 sts). When the center of the work measures 2¼in (6cm), change to no. 2 (3mm) needles and Rich Navy and work ½in (1cm) in K1, P1 rib.* Bind (cast) off loosely.

Front

Work as for the back to *. On the next row bind (cast) off 9 sts at each end (16 sts), then work the bib. Using Rich Navy K1, P1, K1, P1. Change to Ivory and K8. Change to Rich Navy (it is easier to use a separate ball) and K1, P1, K1, P1. Working in rib and st st, with the colors as set, work for a further ¾in (2cm). Keeping the rib as set, work 4 rows in Ivory in garter st. Bind (cast) off the center 8 sts. Cont each strap separately, working in rib as set, until each is 5½in (14cm) long. Bind (cast) off.

Making up

Join the side seams of the shorts. Sow the inner leg and gusset seams together. Use buttonhole cotton to make a button loop at the end of each strap. Stitch the buttons on the back of the shorts.

Child

Shorts

Work the back first. Using no. 2 (3mm) needles and Rich Navy, cast on 38/41 sts. Work 4 rows in garter st. Change to no. 3 (3¼mm) needles and work in st st, inc 1 st at each end of the next row (40/43 sts). Work 2 rows in Ivory, 2 rows in Rich Navy and 2 rows in Ivory. Leave the sts on a spare needle. Work the other leg to match.

Work the gusset. Using no. 3 (3¼mm) needles and Rich Navy, cast on 16 sts. Slip the stitches onto one of the needles between the sts held for the two legs. Work in st st, beg with the 16 sts in the center, picking up on each row 8 sts five times/9 sts three times and 8 sts twice from each group of leg sts. At the same time, on 8 alt rows at the right-hand gusset edge sl1, K1, psso and on the left side K2tog (80/86 sts). When the center of the work measures 6¾/7¼in (17/19cm), change to no. 2 (3mm) needles and work ⅜in (2cm) in K2, P2 rib. Bind (cast) off loosely. Work the front to match.

Join the side seams. Sow the inner leg and gusset seams together. Stitch 2 rows of elastic to the inside of the waistband.

T-shirt front

Using no. 2 (3mm) needles and Red Wine, cast on 72/78 sts. Work 4 rows in garter st. Change to no. 3 (3¼mm) needles and cont in striped st st (working 2 rows in Ivory, 2 rows in Red Wine). When the work measures 6/6¾in (15/17cm) from the beg, work the sleeves, casting on 20 sts at the beg and end of the next row (112/118 sts). Cont in pattern until the work measures 8¼/9½in (21/24cm). Put the center 10/14 sts on a spare needle and work the shoulders separately, binding (casting) off at the neck edge on alt rows 5 sts twice. Using no. 2 (3mm) needles and Red Wine, work 4 rows, including the sts held at the center, in garter st. Bind (cast) off loosely.

T-shirt back

Using no. 2 (3mm) needles and Red Wine, cast on 72/78 sts. Work 4 rows in garter st. Change to no. 3 (3¼mm) needles and cont in striped st st (working 2 rows in Ivory, 2 rows in Red Wine). When the work measures 6/6¾in (15/17cm) from the beg, work the sleeves, casting on 20 sts at the beg and end of the next row (112/118 sts). Cont in pattern until the work measures 9½/10½in (24/27cm). Put the center 10/14 sts on a spare needle and work the shoulders separately, binding (casting) off at the neck edge on alt rows 3 sts twice, 2 sts twice and 1 st three times. Using no. 2 (3mm) needles and

Red Wine, work 4 rows, including the sts held at the center, in garter st. On the second row work 3 evenly spaced buttonholes on each shoulder piece. Bind (cast) off loosely.

Making up

Stitch buttons on the front shoulders to match the buttonholes. Close the side and underarm seams.

Teddy is waiting patiently for his train at the railway station, snugly wrapped up in the duffel coat his mother knitted for him. He is going to stay with his grandmother for a few days. His mother has tucked a scarf into his suitcase as a present for grandmother. The wicker boxes are filled with snacks and some chocolates in case Teddy feels hungry during his journey.

On the Train

Teddy

To fit a bear 13½in (34cm) tall

Wool
*Wendy Aran with Wool (machine washable): 4 balls of
Seascape Tweed (562)*

Needles
*1 pair no. 3 (3¼mm), 1 pair no. 4 (3¾mm) and a spare
needle*

Materials
3 wooden buttons

Stitches
Garter stitch: knit every row
Stockinette (stocking) stitch (st st): knit 1 row, purl 1 row
*Decreasing by 1 st on a knit row: K1, slip the next st onto
the right-hand needle purlwise, K1, pass the slipped stitch
over the knitted st and off the needle (sl1, K1, psso). At
the end of a row, when there are 3 sts on the left-hand
needle, knit 2 sts together (K2tog), K1*
*Decreasing by 2 sts on a knit row: K1, slip the next st
onto the right-hand needle purlwise, knit 2 sts together,
pass the slipped st over the knitted sts off the needle (sl1,
K2tog, psso). At the end of a row, when there are 4 sts on
the left-hand needle, knit 3 sts together (K3tog), K1*

Gauge (Tension)
*Using no. 4 (3¾mm) needles and measured over stockinette
(stocking) stitch, 22 stitches and 28 rows measure 4in
(10cm) square.*

Back

Using no. 3 (3¼mm) needles, cast on 55 sts. Work ¾in (2cm) in garter st. Change to no. 4 (3¾m) needles and cont in st st. When the work measures 4in (10cm) from the beg, work the armhole by dec at each end of alt rows 2 sts once and 1 st once. Then (using sl1, K1 psso), dec 1 st at each end of the next 12 alt rows. At the same time, when the work measures 6½in (17cm) from the beg, bind (cast) off the center 13 sts. Shape the shoulders separately, dec 3 sts twice on alt rows.

Right front

Using no. 3 (3¼mm) needles, cast on 25 sts. Work ¾in (2cm) in garter st. Change to no. 4 (3¾m) needles and cont in st st. When the work measures 2in (5cm) from the beg, work the pocket opening by binding (casting) off the center 9 sts, leaving the remaining sts on a spare needle. Using no. 4 (3¾mm) needles, work the pocket by casting on, separately, 9 sts. Work in st st for 1¼in (3cm) and leave the sts on a spare needle. Using no. 4 (3¾mm) needles, work the pocket flap by casting on, separately, 9 sts. Work 8 rows in garter st. Place the flap against the pocket back, and using no. 3 (3mm) needles knit 1 row, taking 1 st from each piece. Return to the main part of the front, working 8 sts, taking in the 9 sts from the pocket, and working to the end. When the work measures 4in (10cm) from the beg, shape the armhole, by dec at the left-hand side on alt rows 2 sts once and 1 st once. Then (using sl1, K1, psso), dec 1 st at the left-hand end of the next 12 alt rows. At the same time, when the work measure 6½in (17cm) from the beg, bind (cast) off 4 sts once, 2 sts twice and 1 st twice at the right-hand end of alt rows.

Left front

Work as the right front, reversing all shaping.

Sleeves

Using no. 3 (3¼mm) needles, cast on 38 sts. Work ¾in (15mm) in garter st. Change to no. 4 (3¾mm) needles and cont in st st. When the work measures 1½in (4cm) from the beg, bind (cast) off 2 sts once and 1 st once at each end of alt rows. Then (using sl1, K1, psso) dec 1 st ten times and 2 sts three times.

Hood

Using no. 3 (3¼mm) needles, cast on 90 sts. Work 1¼in (3cm) in garter st. Change to no. 4 (3¾mm) needles and cont in st st. When the work measures 6in (15cm) from the beg, bind (cast) off 30 sts at each end. Cont on the center 30 sts until the work measures 11in (28cm). Next row K2tog across the row. Cont until work measures 11½in (29cm). Bind (cast) off.

Making up

Stitch around the pockets.

Using no. 3 (3¼mm) needles make a buttonband by picking up 38 sts up the left front. Work ¾in (2cm) in garter st. Bind (cast) off. On the other front, work a buttonhole band in the same way, making 3 buttonholes, the first 2 sts down from the top, and the others 11 sts apart.

Set in and stitch the armholes. Stitch the side and underarm seams. Attach the hood at the top back and close the top and sides of the hood. Turn back the garter st rows of the hood to make an edging and stitch the bottom to the hood to the front of the jacket. Attach the buttons.

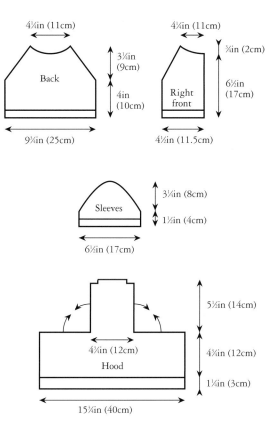

*It is Teddy's birthday and his friends
have bought him some of his favorite
sweets and lollipops. He is going to have
a party, and everyone will hold hands
in a big circle in the garden and sing
"Happy Birthday to You." His mother
has knitted a pretty cardigan with two
hearts on the front. It is his best present.*

Birthday Party

Teddy

To fit a bear 13½in (34cm) tall

Wool
*Wendy Bambine 4-ply (machine washable):
1 ball each of White (1020) and Mint
(1026)*

Needles
*1 pair no 2 (3mm), 1 pair no 3 (3¼mm)
and a darning needle*

Materials
2 small mother-of-pearl buttons

Stitches
*Rib: K1, P1
Stockinette (stocking) stitch (st st): knit 1
row, purl 1 row
Cross stitch: follow the chart opposite*

Gauge (Tension)
*Using no. 3 (3¼mm) needles and measured
over stockinette (stocking) stitch, 30 stitches
and 41 rows measure 4in (10cm) square.*

Child

To fit a child 3/6 months

Wool
*Wendy Bambine 4-ply (machine washable):
3/4 balls of White (1020) and 1 ball of
Mint (1026)*

Needles
*1 pair no 2 (3mm), 1 pair no 3 (3¼mm)
and a darning needle*

Materials
2 small mother-of-pearl buttons

Stitches
*Rib: K1, P1
Stockinette (stocking) stitch (st st): knit 1
row, purl 1 row
Cross stitch: follow the chart opposite*

Gauge (Tension)
*Using no. 3 (3¼mm) needles and measured
over stockinette (stocking) stitch, 30 stitches
and 41 rows measure 4in (10cm) square.*

Child

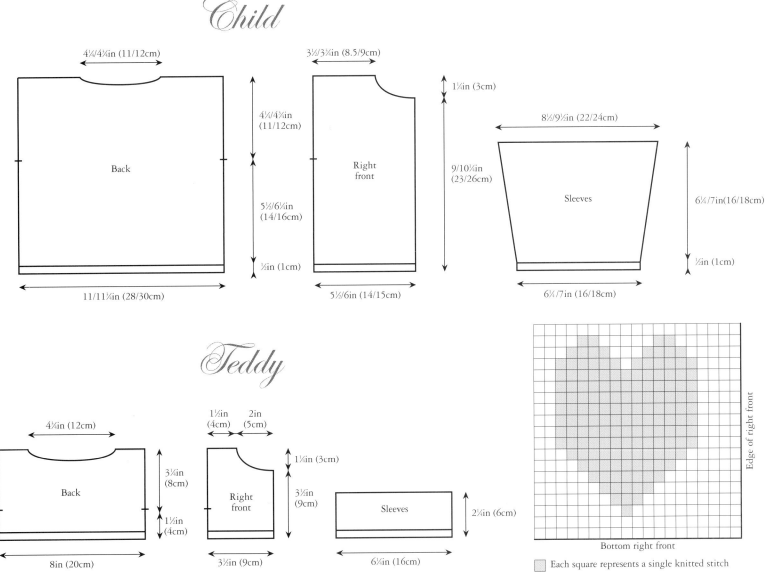

Back

4¼/4¾in (11/12cm)

4¼/4¾in (11/12cm)

5½/6¼in (14/16cm)

½in (1cm)

11/11¾in (28/30cm)

Right front

3½/3¾in (8.5/9cm)

1⅛in (3cm)

9/10¼in (23/26cm)

5½/6in (14/15cm)

Sleeves

8½/9½in (22/24cm)

6¼/7in (16/18cm)

½in (1cm)

6¼/7in (16/18cm)

Teddy

Back

4¾in (12cm)

3¼in (8cm)

1½in (4cm)

8in (20cm)

Right front

1½in (4cm) 2in (5cm)

1⅛in (3cm)

3½in (9cm)

3½in (9cm)

Sleeves

2¼in (6cm)

6¼in (16cm)

Edge of right front

Bottom right front

☐ Each square represents a single knitted stitch

Birthday Party

Teddy

Back

Using no. 2 (3mm) needles and Mint, cast on 75 sts. Work in K1, P1 rib for ½in (1cm), dec 15 sts evenly across the last row (60 sts). Change to no. 3 (3¼mm) needles and White and work in st st. When the work measures 4½in (11cm) from the beg, bind (cast) off the center 14 sts and work each side separately. Shape the neck by binding (casting) off 5 sts twice on alt rows (13 sts). When the work measures 4¾in (12cm) from the beg, bind (cast) off loosely.

Right front

Using no. 2 (3mm) needles and Mint, cast on 35 sts. Work in K1, P1 rib for ½in (1cm), dec 7 sts evenly across the last row (28 sts). Change to no. 3 (3¼mm) needles and White and work in st st. When the work measures 3½in (9cm) from the beg, shape the neck by binding (casting) off 5 sts once, 4 sts once, 3 sts once and 1 st three times on alt rows (13 sts). When the work measures 4¾in (12cm) from the beg, bind (cast) off loosely.

Left front

Work as for the right front but reversing all shaping.

Sleeves

Using no. 2 (3mm) needles and Mint, cast on 63 sts. Work in K1, P1 rib for ½in (1cm), dec 13 sts evenly across the last row (50 sts). Change to no. 3 (3¼mm) needles and White and work in st st. When the work measures 2¼in (6cm) from the beg, bind (cast) off loosely. Work another sleeve to match.

Making up

Stitch the shoulder seams together. To make the neckband, use no. 2 (3mm) needles and Mint. Pick up 101 sts from around the top and work in K1, P1 rib for ½in (1cm). Bind (cast) off.

To make the buttonband, use no. 2 (3mm) needles and Mint. Pick up 47 sts from the edge of the left front and work in K1, P1 rib for ½in (1cm). Bind (cast) off. Make the buttonhole band in the same way along the edge of the right front, but making 2 small buttonholes, the first 2 sts from the top, the second 7 sts from the first.

Using Mint and a darning needle, follow the chart to embroider the hearts on the left and right fronts. Work in cross stitch, covering a single knitted stitch with each embroidery stitch and positioning the hearts as indicated on the chart.

Set in the sleeves, easing them around the shoulder. Join the side and underarm seams. Stitch on the buttons.

Child

Back

Using no. 2 (3mm) needles and Mint, cast on 101/107 sts. Work in K1, P1 rib for ½in (1cm), dec 15 sts evenly across the last row (86/92 sts). Change to no. 3 (3¼mm) needles and White and work in st st. When the work measures 9¾/11in (25/28cm) from the beg, bind (cast) off the center 14/18 sts and work each side separately. Shape the neck by binding (casting) off 5 sts twice on alt rows (26/27 sts). When the work measures 10¼/11½in (26/29cm) from the beg, bind (cast) off loosely.

Right front

Using no. 2 (3mm) needles and Mint, cast on 50/53 sts. Work in K1, P1 rib for ½in (1cm), dec 7 sts evenly across the last row (43/46 sts). Change to no. 3 (3¼mm) needles and White and work in st st. When the work measures 9/10¼in (23/26cm) from the beg, shape the neck by binding (casting) off 8/9 sts once, 5/6 sts once, 2/2 sts once and 1/1 st twice on alt rows (26/27 sts). When the work measures 10¼/11½in (26/29cm) from the beg, bind (cast) off loosely.

Left front

Work as for the right front but reversing all shaping.

Sleeves

Using no. 2 (3mm) needles and Mint, cast on 66/70 sts. Work in K1, P1 rib for ½in (1cm), dec 13 sts evenly across the last row (53/57 sts). Change to no. 3 (3¼mm) needles and White and work in st st, increasing 1 st 7/8 times at both ends of the every eighth row (67/73 sts). When the work measures 6¼/7½in (17/19cm) from the beg, bind (cast) off loosely. Work another sleeve to match.

Making up

Stitch the shoulder seams together. To make the neckband, use no. 2 (3mm) needles and Mint. Pick up 101/109 sts from around the top and work in K1, P1 rib for ½in (1cm). Bind (cast) off.

To make the buttonband, use no. 2 (3mm) needles and Mint. Pick up 93/105 sts from the edge of the left front and work in K1, P1 rib for ½in (1cm). Bind (cast) off. Make the buttonhole band in the same way along the edge of the right front, but making 2 small buttonholes, the first 2 sts from the top, the second 25 sts from the first.

Using Mint and a darning needle, follow the chart to embroider the hearts on the left and right fronts. Work in cross stitch, covering a single knitted stitch with each embroidery stitch and positioning the hearts as indicated on the chart.

Set in the sleeves, easing them around the shoulder. Join the side and underarm seams. Stitch on the buttons.

It is time to go back to school today, and Teddy is wearing a special sweater that his mother has knitted for him. It has got a pattern of pencils across the front. He will use a pencil to draw some flowers, dragonflies and ladybirds. He will also be able to write on his new chalkboard, but for the moment he would far rather play with his spinning tops and dream about having fun with his friends.

At School

Teddy

To fit a bear 13½in (34cm) tall

Wool
Wendy Courtelle Double Knit (machine washable): 1 ball each of Aran (90), Orange (128), Emerald (121), Cherry Red (84) and Royal (86)

Needles
1 pair no. 2 (3mm) and 1 pair no. 3 (3¼mm)

Materials
6 pencil-shaped buttons
1 strip of Velcro, 4in (10cm) long

Stitches
Rib: K1, P1
Stockinette (stocking) stitch (st st): knit 1 row, purl 1 row

Gauge (Tension)
Using no. 3 (3¼mm) needles and measured over stockinette (stocking) stitch, 24 stitches and 31 rows measure 4in (10cm) square.

Child

To fit a child 3/6 months

Wool
Wendy Courtelle Double Knit (machine washable): 2 balls each of Aran (90) and Cherry Red (84); 1 ball each of Orange (128), Emerald (121) and Royal (86)

Needles
1 pair no. 2 (3mm) and 1 pair no. 3 (3¼mm)

Materials
6 pencil-shaped button
6 small buttons

Stitches
Rib: K1, P1
Stockinette (stocking) stitch (st st): knit 1 row, purl 1 row

Gauge (Tension)
Using no. 3 (3¼mm) needles and measured over stockinette (stocking) stitch, 24 stitches and 31 rows measure 4in (10cm) square

Teddy

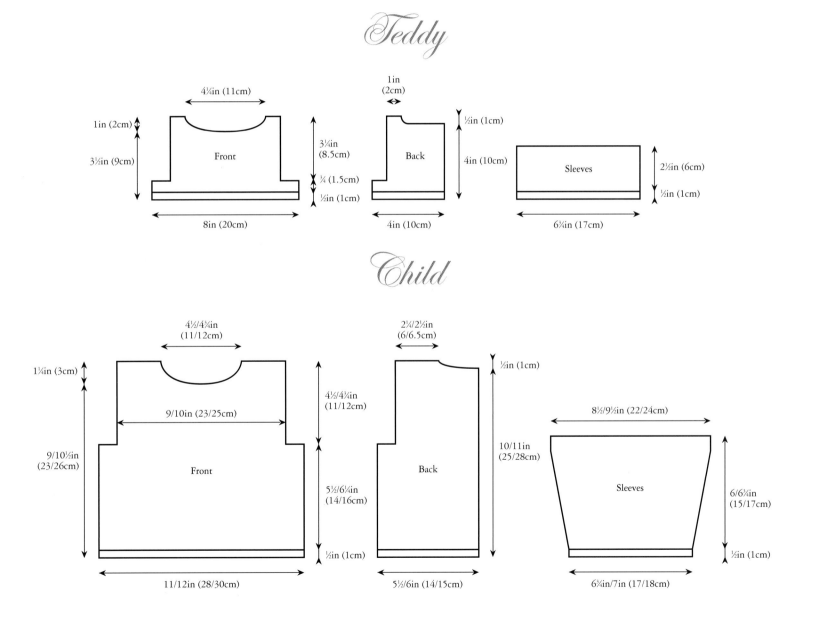

4¼in (11cm)

1in
(2cm)

1in (2cm)

3½in (9cm)

Front

3¼in
(8.5cm)

¾ (1.5cm)

½in (1cm)

8in (20cm)

Back

½in (1cm)

4in (10cm)

4in (10cm)

Sleeves

2½in (6cm)

½in (1cm)

6¾in (17cm)

Child

4½/4¾in
(11/12cm)

1¼in (3cm)

2¼/2½in
(6/6.5cm)

½in (1cm)

9/10in (23/25cm)

4½/4¾in
(11/12cm)

9/10½in
(23/26cm)

Front

5½/6¼in
(14/16cm)

Back

10/11in
(25/28cm)

½in (1cm)

8½/9½in (22/24cm)

Sleeves

6/6¾in
(15/17cm)

½in (1cm)

11/12in (28/30cm)

5½/6in (14/15cm)

6¾in/7in (17/18cm)

Teddy

Front

Using no. 2 (3mm) needles and Orange, cast on 50 sts. Work in K1, P1 rib for ½in (1cm). Change to no. 3 (3¼mm) needles and Cherry Red, and cont in st st until work measures 1¼in (2.5cm) from beg. Shape the armholes by binding (casting) off 6 sts at the beg and end of the next row (38 sts). Cont in st st until the work measures 1½in (3.5cm). Cont in st st, work 2 rows in Aran, 1 row in Royal, 2 rows in Aran, 1 row in Orange, 2 rows in Aran and 1 row in Emerald. Cont in Aran until work measures 3½in (9cm) from beg. Shape the neck front by binding (casting) off the central 14 sts. Work each shoulder separately. On alternate rows at the shoulder edge dec 3 sts, 2 sts and 1 st (6 sts). Cont in st st until work measures 4½in (11cm) from beg. Bind (cast) off.

Back

Using no. 2 (3mm) needles and Orange, cast on 25 sts. Work in K1, P1 rib for ½in (1cm). Change to no. 3 (3¼mm) needles and Cherry Red and cont as for the front until work measures 1¼in (2.5cm) from beg. Shape the left armhole by binding (casting) off 6 sts (19 sts). Cont in st st until work measures 4in (10cm) from beg. Shape neck at right of work by dec on alternate rows 8 sts, 4 sts and 1 st (6 sts). Cont in st st until work measures 4½in (11cm) from beg. Bind (cast) off. Work the other half of back to match the first, reversing all shapings.

Right sleeve

Using no. 2 (3mm) needles and Orange, cast on 42 sts. Work in K1, P1 rib for ½in (1cm). Change to no. 3 (3.25mm) needles and cont in st st, working 2 rows in Royal and 1 row in Orange. Using Royal, cont in st st until sleeve measures 3in (7cm) from beg. Bind (cast) off.

Left sleeve

Work as for the right sleeve but using Emerald instead of Royal.

Making up

Stitch the shoulder seams together. Using no. 2 (3mm) needles and Aran, pick up 73 sts around the neck. Work the neckband in K1, P1 rib for ½in (1cm).

Using no. 2 (3mm) needles and Aran pick up 43 sts up the inside back. Work the back band in K1, P1 rib for ½in (1cm). Repeat on the other side of the back opening.

Set in and stitch each sleeve seam. Stitch the side and under-arm seams. Attach the Velcro to the back opening. Stitch the pencil buttons across the front of the sweater.

Child

Front

Using no. 2 (3mm) needles and Orange, cast on 68/74 sts. Work in K1, P1 rib for ½in (1cm). Change to no. 3 (3¼mm) needles and Cherry Red and cont in st st. When work measures 6/6¾in (15/17cm) from the beg, shape the armholes by binding (casting) off 6 sts at the beg and end of the next row (56/62 sts). Cont in st st until the work measures 6¼/7in (16/18cm) from the beg. Work 2 rows in Aran, 1 row in Royal, 2 rows in Aran, 1 row in Orange, 2 rows in Aran and 1 row in Emerald.

Using Aran, cont in st st until work measures 9/10½in (23/26cm) from beg. Shape neck by binding (casting) off central 14/16 sts (42/46 sts). Work each shoulder separately. On alternate rows at the shoulder edge dec 3 sts, 2 sts, 1 st and 1 st (14/16 sts). Cont in st st until work measures 10¼/11¾in (26/29cm) from beg. Bind (cast) off.

Back

Using no. 2 (3mm) needles and Orange, cast on 34/37 sts. Work in K1, P1 rib for ½in (1cm). Change to no. 3 (3¼mm) needles and Cherry Red and cont in st st as for the front until work measures 6/6¾in (15/17cm) from the beg. Shape left armhole by binding (casting) off 6 sts at beg of next row (28/31 sts). Cont in st st until work measures 10/11in (25/28cm) from the beg. Shape neck at right of work by dec on alt rows 7/8 sts and 7/7 sts (14/16 sts). Cont in st st until work measures 10½/11½in (26/29cm) from beg. Bind (cast) off.

Work the other half of back to match the first, reversing all shapings.

Right sleeve

Using no. 2 (3mm) needles and Orange, cast on 40/44 sts. Work in K1, P1 rib for ½in (1cm). Change to no. 3 (3¼mm) needles and cont in st st, working 2 rows in Royal and 1 row in Orange. Using Royal, cont in st st, inc 1 st at each end of every following sixth row 6/7 times

(52/58 sts). Work until sleeve measures 6½/7¼in (16/18cm) from beg. Bind (cast) off.

Left sleeve

Work as for the right sleeve but using Emerald instead of Royal.

Making up

Stitch the shoulder seams together. Using no. 2 (3mm) needles and Aran, pick up 73 sts around the neck. Work the neckband in K1, P1 rib for ½in (1cm).

Using no. 2 (3mm) needles and Aran pick up 73/83 sts along the inside back. Work the back band in K1, P1 rib for ½in (1cm). At the same time, work 6 small buttonholes, the first 3 sts from the top, the remainder spaced evenly 12/14 sts apart. Repeat on the other side of the back opening, omitting the buttonholes.

Set in and stitch each sleeve seam. Stitch the side and under-arm seams. Attach the six buttons to match the positions of the buttonholes on the back opening. Stitch the pencil buttons across the front of the sweater.

Teddy is staying on grandfather's farm for a holiday, and he is waiting in a corner of the shed while his grandmother is milking Buttercup the cow. He is wearing his warm Aran sweater, which his mother has knitted for him. Before he goes to bed tonight he will drink some delicious hot chocolate, made with fresh, creamy milk.

On the Farm

Teddy

To fit a bear 13½in (34cm) tall

Wool
Sunbeam St Ives 4-ply (machine washable): 1 ball of Oatmeal (3002)

Needles
1 pair no. 2 (3mm), 1 pair no. 3 (3¼mm), 1 cable needle

Materials
1 strip of Velcro, 4in (10cm) long

Stitches
Rib: K1, P1
Double seed (moss) stitch (worked over 4 rows and an even number of sts): Row 1: K1, P1 to end; Row 2: K1, P1 to end; Row 3: P1, K1 to end; Row 4: P1, K1 to end
Cable pattern (worked over 12 rows and 32 sts): see chart opposite

Gauge (Tension)
Using no. 3 (3¼mm) needles and measured over double seed (moss) stitch, 28 sts and 36 rows measure 4in (10cm) square.

Child

To fit a child 3/6 months

Wool
Sunbeam St Ives 4-ply (machine washable): 4/5 balls of Oatmeal (3002)

Needles
1 pair no. 2 (3mm), 1 pair no. 3 (3¼mm), 1 cable needle

Materials
6 small cream-colored buttons

Stitches
Rib: K1, P1
Double seed (moss) stitch (worked over 4 rows and an even number of sts): Row 1: K1, P1 to end; Row 2: K1, P1 to end; Row 3: P1, K1 to end; Row 4: P1, K1 to end
Cable pattern (worked over 12 rows and 32 sts): see chart opposite

Gauge (Tension)
Using no. 3 (3¼mm) needles and measured over double seed (moss) stitch, 28 sts and 36 rows measure 4in (10cm) square.

Hat

To fit a bear 13½in (34cm) tall or child 3/6 months

Wool
Sunbeam St Ives 4-ply (machine washable): 1 ball of Oatmeal (3002)

Needles
1 pair no. 2 (3mm), 1 cable needle

Stitches
Rib: K1, P1
Double seed (moss) stitch (worked over 4 rows and an even number of sts): Row 1: K1, P1 to end; Row 2: K1, P1 to end; Row 3: P1, K1 to end; Row 4: P1, K1 to end
Cable pattern: worked over the first 10 sts and all 12 rows of the chart

Gauge (Tension)
Using no. 2 (3mm) needles and measured over double seed (moss) stitch, 32 sts and 42 rows measure 4in (10cm) square.

Teddy

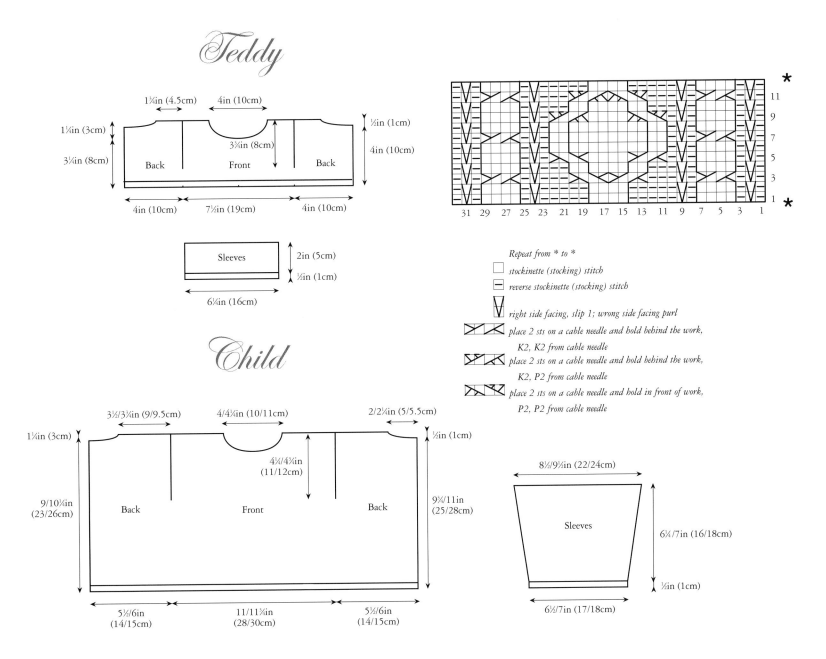

1¾in (4.5cm)

4in (10cm)

1¼in (3cm)

3¼in (8cm)

Back

3⅛in (8cm)

Front

½in (1cm)

4in (10cm)

Back

4in (10cm)

7½in (19cm)

4in (10cm)

Sleeves

2in (5cm)

½in (1cm)

6¼in (16cm)

Repeat from * to *

☐ stockinette (stocking) stitch

⊟ reverse stockinette (stocking) stitch

V right side facing, slip 1; wrong side facing purl

place 2 sts on a cable needle and hold behind the work, K2, K2 from cable needle

place 2 sts on a cable needle and hold behind the work, K2, P2 from cable needle

place 2 sts on a cable needle and hold in front of work, P2, P2 from cable needle

Child

3½/3¾in (9/9.5cm)

4/4¼in (10/11cm)

2/2¼in (5/5.5cm)

1¼in (3cm)

4¼/4¾in (11/12cm)

½in (1cm)

9/10¼in (23/26cm)

Back

Front

Back

9¾/11in (25/28cm)

5½/6in (14/15cm)

11/11¾in (28/30cm)

5½/6in (14/15cm)

8½/9½in (22/24cm)

Sleeves

6¼/7in (16/18cm)

½in (1cm)

6½/7in (17/18cm)

Teddy

Front and back

The body of the sweater is worked as a single piece, beg at the bottom. Using no. 2 (3mm) needles, cast on 109 sts. Work in K1, P1 rib for ½in (1cm). Change to no. 3 (3¼mm) needles and work as follows. Next row, inc by 3 sts evenly across row and at the same time, work in double seed (moss) st for 40 sts, beg to follow chart for 32 sts, work in double seed (moss) st for 40 sts (112 sts). Cont in pattern as set until the work measures 1¼in (3cm) from the beg, then work only on the first 28 sts to complete the right back.

When the work measures 4in (10cm) from the beg, shape the neck by binding (casting) off 16 sts. Cont in pattern as set until the work measures 4½in (11cm), then bind (cast) off the remaining 12 sts.

Complete the front by picking up the 56 sts in the center and working in pattern as set until the work measures 3¼in (8cm). Bind (cast) off the center 12 sts for the neck and work on each side separately. Shape the neck by binding (casting) off 4 sts once, 2 sts twice and 1 st twice on alt rows (12 sts). When the work measures 4½in (11cm) from the beg, bind (cast) off the remaining 12 sts at the shoulder.

Pick up the remaining 28 sts and work the left back as before, reversing all shaping and keeping in pattern as set.

Sleeves

Using no. 2 (3mm) needles, cast on 45 sts. Work in K1, P1 rib for ½in (1cm). Change to no. 3 (3¼mm) needles and work as follows. Next row, inc by 1 st in the center of the row and at the same time, work in double seed (moss) st for 18 sts, work the first 10 sts from the chart, work in double seed (moss) st for 18 sts (46 sts). When the work measures 2½in (6cm) from the beg, bind (cast) off. Work the other sleeve to match.

Making up

Stitch the shoulder seams. Make a neckband. Using no. 2 (3mm) needles pick up 75 sts around the neck and work in K1, P1 rib for ½in (1cm). Bind (cast) off loosely.

Make a band up both back openings, using no. 2 (3mm) needles and picking up 75 sts. Work in K1, P1 rib for ½in (1cm) on both sides. Stitch the underarm seams and set in the sleeves, easing them to fit. Attach the Velcro to the back opening.

Child

Front and back

The body of the sweater is worked as a single piece, beg at the bottom. Using no. 2 (3mm) needles, cast on 149/161 sts. Work in K1, P1 rib for ½in (1cm). Change to no. 3 (3¼mm) needles and work as follows. Next row, inc by 3 sts evenly across row and at the same time, work in double seed (moss) st for 60/66 sts, beg to follow chart for 32 sts, work in double seed (moss) st for 60/66 sts (152/164 sts). Cont in pattern as set until the work measures 6/6¾in (15/17cm) from the beg, then work only on the first 40/43 sts to complete the right back.

When the work measures 9¾/11in (25/28cm) from the beg, shape the neck by binding (casting) off 8/9 sts once and 7/8 sts once on alt rows (25/26 sts). Cont in pattern as set until the work measures 10¼/11½in (26/29cm), then bind (cast) off the remaining 25/26 sts.

Complete the front by picking up the 72/78 sts in the center and working in pattern as set until the work measures 9/10¼in (23/26cm). Bind (cast) off the center 8/12 sts for the neck and work on each side separately. Shape the neck by binding (casting) off 3/3 sts once, 2/2 sts once and 1/1 st twice on alt rows (25/26 sts). When the work measures 10¼/11½in (26/29cm) from the beg, bind (cast) off the remaining 25/26 sts at the shoulder.

Pick up the remaining 40/43 sts and work the left back as before, reversing all shaping and keeping in pattern as set.

Sleeves

Using no. 2 (3mm) needles, cast on 49/53 sts. Work in K1, P1 rib for ½in (1cm). Change to no. 3 (3¼mm) needles and work as follows. Next row, inc by 1 st in the center of the row and at the same time, work in double seed (moss) st for 20/22 sts, work the first 10 sts from the chart, work in double seed (moss) st for 20/22 sts (50/54 sts). Inc by 1 st at each end of every eighth row 7/8 times (64/70 sts). When the work measures 6¾/7½in (17/19cm) from the beg, bind (cast) off. Work the other sleeve to match.

Making up

Stitch the shoulder seams. Make a neckband. Using no. 2 (3mm) needles pick up 75/81 sts around the neck and work in K1, P1 rib for ½in (1cm). Bind (cast) off loosely.

Make a buttonband up one back opening, using no. 2 (3mm) needles and picking up 73/83 sts. Work in K1, P1 rib for ½in (1cm). Make a buttonhole band on the other side of the back opening to match the buttonband, but working 6 evenly spaced buttonholes, the first 3 sts from the top. Stitch the underarm seams and set in the sleeves, easing them to fit. Stitch the buttons in place on the buttonband to match the buttonholes.

Hat

The materials and instructions given will make a hat that will fit a bear 13½in (34cm) tall; the sizes given after the oblique are for a small child of 3 to 6 months.

Using no. 2 (3mm) needles, cast on 122/152 sts. Work in K1, P1 rib for ¾in (2cm). Next row: K1, *work first 10 sts from chart, work 11/16 sts in double seed (moss) st*, rep from * to * 6 times, K1. At the same time, inc by 1 st in the center of each of the six cable sections (128/158).

When the work measures 3½/4½in (9/11cm) from the beg, dec in the double seed (moss) st sections 1 st twice every

fourth row. Then dec by 1 st on alt rows until one 1 st remains between slipped sts. Beg to dec the cable pattern by K2tog on every row. Use a crochet hook to pull the

yarn through the remaining sts and close the seam. Make a pompon for the top, following the instruction given in the next pattern, *In the Country*.

Teddy has been to the forest to collect some pine cones, and he has been wearing his smart Tyrolean-style jacket and hat to keep him warm. He and his friends are going to decorate the cones with red ribbon and gold paint and use them to brighten up the supper table.

Knitting for Teddies

Teddy

To fit a bear 13½in (34cm) tall

Wool
*Wendy Guernsey 5-ply (hand wash only): 2
balls of Crimson (590) and 1 ball of
Atlantic Blue (674)*

Needles
*1 pair no. 2 (3mm) needles, 1 pair no. 3
(3¼mm) needles and 1 no. 2 crochet hook*

Materials
7 metal buttons

Stitches
*Stockinette (stocking) stitch (st st): knit 1
row, purl 1 row*
*Reverse stockinette (stocking) stitch: with
right side facing, purl 1 row, knit 1 row*
Crochet: basic chain and double crochet

Gauge (Tension)
*Using no. 3 (3¼mm) needles and measured
over reverse stockinette (stocking) stitch, 28 sts
and 44 rows measure 4in (10cm) square.*

Teddy

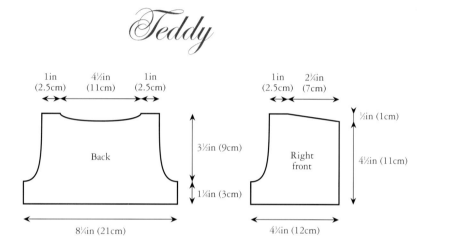

1in (2.5cm)   4½in (11cm)   1in (2.5cm)

Back

3½in (9cm)

1¼in (3cm)

8¼in (21cm)

1in (2.5cm)   2¾in (7cm)

½in (1cm)

Right front

4½in (11cm)

4¾in (12cm)

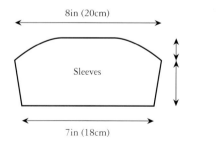

8in (20cm)

Sleeves

7in (18cm)

Pockets

1¼in (3cm)

1½in (4cm)

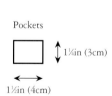

Making a pompom

Use a pair of compasses to draw two circles on a piece of card. Make a hole in the center of each. Thread wool around the card circles, taking it through the center and working evenly around the card. When you can get no more wool through the hole, use a pair of sharp scissors to cut through the wool between the two card circles. Before you remove the card, fasten a piece of wool around the pompom and between the card circles, fastening it tightly. Remove the card and clip the surface of the pompom to neaten it.

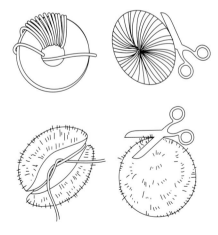

Teddy

Back

Using no. 3 (3¼mm) and Atlantic Blue, cast on 60 sts and work in reverse st st. When the work measures 1¼in (3cm) from the beg, shape the armholes by binding (casting) off 4 sts once, 2 sts once and 1 st twice at each end of alt rows (44 sts). When the work measures 4½in (11cm) from the beg, bind (cast) off the center 8 sts and complete each side separately, shaping the neck by binding (casting) off 5 sts twice on alt rows (8 sts). Cont on these sts until the work measures 4¾in (12cm) from the beg. Bind (cast) off. Complete the other side to match, reversing all shaping.

Right front

Using no. 3 (3¼mm) needles and Atlantic Blue, cast on 34 sts and work in reverse st st. When the work measures 1¼in (3cm) from the beg, shape the armhole as for the back (26 sts). When the work measures 4½in (11cm) from the beg, work the jacket lapel by binding (casting) off 9 sts twice on alt rows (8 sts). Cont on these sts until the work measures 4¾in (12cm) from the beg. Bind (cast) off.

Left front

Work to match the right front, but reversing all shaping. When the work measures ½in (1cm), 1¼in (3cm) and 2in (5cm) from the bottom, work buttonholes 3 sts in from the front edge.

Sleeves

Using no. 3 (3¼mm) needles and Atlantic Blue, cast on 50 sts and work in reverse st st, inc by 1 st at each end of every sixth row three times (56 sts). When the work measures 2½in (6cm) from the beg, bind (cast) off 4 sts once, 2 sts three times, 3 sts once and 4 sts once at each end of alt rows (22 sts). Bind (cast) off. Work the other sleeve to match.

Pockets

Using no. 3 (3¼mm) needles and Atlantic Blue, cast on 12 sts. Work in reverse st st until the work measures 1¼in (3cm) from the beg. Bind (cast) off. Work the other pocket to match.

Making up

Join the shoulder seams. Set in the sleeves. Join the side and underarm seams. Use a piece of colored cotton to mark the beg of the lapel 2½in (6cm) up from the bottom of each front. Using Crimson, edge the entire jacket with a border of crochet, taking 1 st every knitted st or 1 st every 2 rows. Work on the right side of the back, the back of the collar and bottom of the front and up the first 2½in (6cm) of the front up to the turn of the revers. Work on the wrong side for the lapel, working 3 sts at the corner. Work a second row of crochet all round. Edge the cuffs and the pocket tops in the same way. Stitch the pockets in place.

Attach three buttons to match the button holes. Fold back the lapels and keep them in place by stitching buttons through both layers.

Hat

Using no. 3 (3¼mm) needles and Atlantic Blue, cast on 98 sts. Work in st st until the work measures 7in (18cm) from the beg.

Change to no. 2 (3mm) needles and begin to shape the point of the hat. Next row: *K4, K2tog*, rep from * to * to end. Repeat this row four times every sixth row. Next row: *K2, K2tog*, rep from * to * to end. Repeat this row three times every fourth row. Slip the yarn through the remaining sts and fasten off.

Join the seam, stitching on the outside for the bottom 2½in (6cm) and on the inside up to the top. Crochet two rows in Crimson around the bottom edge. Turn up the bottom 1¼in (3in) and catch it in position.

Make two Crimson pompoms. Attach these with cord to the top of the hat. Bend over the top and catch it in place to one side with one or two small stitches on the inside.

Knitting for Teddies

Mother Bear and Baby Bear have gone away to the mountains for their winter holiday, and Mother Bear hopes to go skiing while Baby Bear has fun with his toboggan. They are both wearing their warmest clothes, and Mother Bear has also packed her scarf and matching shoes.

Sweater and hat to fit a bear 13½ in (34cm) tall

Wool
Wendy DK (machine washable): 3 balls of Splash Blue (534) and 1 ball of White (466)

Needles
1 pair of no. 3 (3¼mm), 1 pair of no. 4 (3¾mm) and a darning needle

Materials
1 strip of Velcro, 4in (10cm) long

Stitches
Rib: K2, P2
Stockinette (stocking) stitch (st st): knit 1 row, purl 1 row
Swiss darning: on the finished sweater cover individual knitted stitches with V-shaped stitches worked in wool of a similar weight to the garment
Simple decrease: on a knit row decrease 2 sts by slipping the next st purlwise onto the right-hand needle, knit the next 2 sts tog, then pass the slipped st over the knitted st and off the needle (sl1, K2tog, psso)

Gauge (Tension)
Using no. 4 (3¾mm) needles and measured over stockinette (stocking) stitch, 20 stitches and 26 rows measure 4in (10cm) square.

Scarf and shoes to fit a bear 13½ in (34cm) tall

Wool
Wendy DK (machine washable): 1 ball Splash Blue (534)
Wendy Rembrandt DK (machine washable): 1 ball Diamond White (3501)

Needles
1 pair of no. 2 (3mm) and spare needles (or safety pins)

Stitches
Rib: K1, P1
Stockinette (stocking) stitch (st st): knit 1 row, purl 1 row
Reverse stockinette (stocking) stitch: with right side facing, purl 1 row, knit 1 row

Gauge (Tension)
Using no. 3 (3¼mm) needles and measured over stockinette (stocking) stitch, 24 stitches and 34 rows measure 4in (10cm) square.

To fit a bear 9½in (24cm) tall

Wool
Wendy Bambine 4-ply (machine washable): 1 ball Powder (1027)
Wendy Rembrandt DK (machine washable): 1 ball Diamond White (3501)

Needles
1 pair no. 3 (3¼mm), 1 pair no. 4 (3¾mm) and a spare needle

Materials
3 small mother-of-pearl buttons
1 strip of narrow Velcro, 4in (10cm) long

Stitches
Garter stitch: knit every row
Stockinette (stocking) stitch (st st): knit 1 row, purl 1 row

Gauge (Tension)
Using no. 4 (3¾mm) needles and measured over stockinette (stocking) stitch, 18 stitches and 24 rows measure 4in (10cm) square.

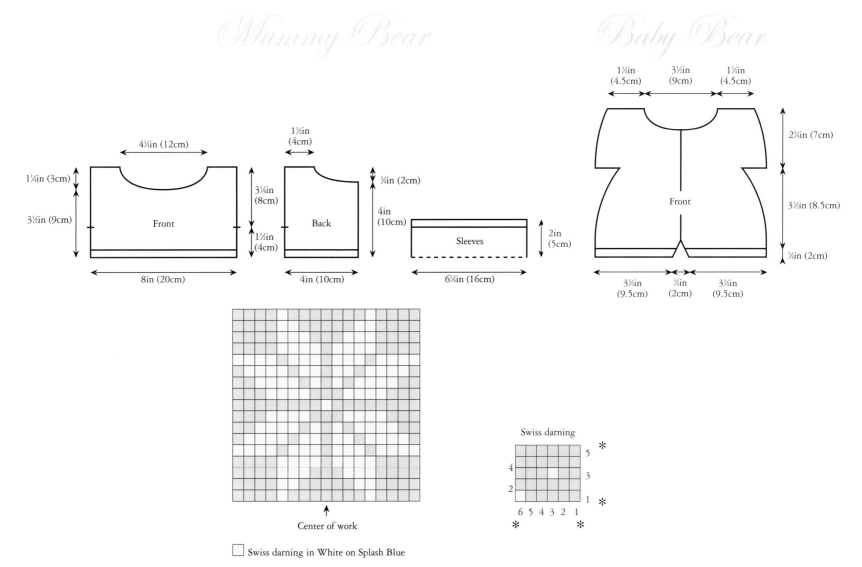

Mummy Bear

Baby Bear

4¾in (12cm)

1½in
(4cm)

1⅛in (3cm)

3½in (9cm)

Front

3¼in
(8cm)

1½in
(4cm)

Back

¾in (2cm)

4in
(10cm)

Sleeves

2in
(5cm)

8in (20cm)

4in (10cm)

6¼in (16cm)

1¾in
(4.5cm)

3½in
(9cm)

1¾in
(4.5cm)

2¾in (7cm)

Front

3⅜in (8.5cm)

¾in (2cm)

3¾in
(9.5cm)

¾in
(2cm)

3¾in
(9.5cm)

↑

Center of work

Swiss darning

5 ✳

4   3

2   1 ✳

6 5 4 3 2 1

✳   ✳

□ Swiss darning in White on Splash Blue

Mummy Bear

Front

Using no. 3 (3¼mm) needles and Splash Blue, cast on 42 sts. Work 5 rows in K2, P2 rib. Change to no. 4 (3¾in) needles and st st. When the work measures 3½in (9cm) from the beg, bind (cast) off the center 10 sts and work each side separately. Shape the shoulder by binding (casting) off 2 sts twice and 1 st three times on alt rows (9 sts). Continue until the work measures 4¾in (12cm) from the beg. Bind (cast) off. Work the other shoulder to match, reversing the shaping.

Back

Using no. 3 (3¼mm) needles and Splash Blue, cast on 22 sts. Work 5 rows in K2, P2 rib. Change to no. 4 (3¾in) needles and st st. When the work measures 4in (10cm) from the beg, shape the neck, binding (casting) off 7 sts once and 3 sts twice on alt rows (9 sts). Continue until the work measures 4¾in (12cm) from the beg. Bind (cast) off. Work the other side to match, reversing the shaping.

Sleeves

Join the shoulder seams. Using no. 4 (3¾mm) needles and Splash Blue, pick up 17 sts over 3¼in (8cm) of each armhole (34 sts). Work in st st for 1½in (4cm). Change to no. 3 (3¼mm) needles and work 5 rows in K2, P2 rib. Bind (cast) off. Make the other sleeve in the same way.

Making up

Join the side and underarm seams. Follow the chart and embroider the snowflake motif on the front of the sweater, using Swiss darning and White.

Make the neckband. Using no. 3 (3¼mm) needles and Splash Blue, pick up 78 sts from around the neck. Work 10 rows in K2, KP rib. Bind (cast) off loosely. Turn over the collar. Attach the Velcro strip to the back.

Hat

Using no. 3 (3¼in) needles and Splash Blue, cast on 106 sts. Work 3¼in (8cm) in K2, P2 rib, dec 2 sts in last row (104 sts). Change to no. 4 (3¾mm) needles and st st. Next row: sl1, *K14, sl1, K2tog, psso*, rep from * to * six times, sl1. Repeat the previous row, keeping decreases above each other, three times every six rows, twice every 4 rows and once more after 2 rows. Next row: sl1, K2tog, psso, sl1. Slip the wool through the sts left and pull the top of the hat to a point. Join the seam with back stitch. Follow the small chart to Swiss darn flakes of snow in White. Turn up the bottom of the hat.

Scarf

Using no. 2 (3mm) needles and Diamond White, cast on 13 sts. Work in K1, P1 rib for 32in (80cm). Bind (cast) off. Gather the ends slightly and make two pompoms from Splash Blue to attach to the ends.

Shoes

Begin work on the upper part of the shoe. Using no. 2 (3mm) needles and Diamond White, cast on 40 sts. Work 5 rows in reverse st st. Change to Splash Blue and st st. On the fourth row work 4 inc into the center 8 sts (44 sts). Work 6 more rows. Leaving the 16 sts at each end on spare needles or safety pins, work on the 12 center sts only. Cont in st st to make the sole of the shoe. On the 12th and 14th rows of the sole, dec 1 st at each end of 2 rows (8 sts). Leave these sts on a spare needle or safety pin.

Change to Diamond White. Pick up 10 sts from the edge of each side of the sole with the 8 held sts in the center (28 sts). Work 4 rows in reverse st st. Pick up all held sts (60 sts). On the wrong side of the work, using a fine needle, pick up each st from the cast-on row. Work in st st and Splash Blue, beginning with 2 purl rows, and knitting together, on the first row, the picked-up sts and the corresponding sts on the left-hand needle to make the side. Decrease by 1 st 16 sts in from each end on 4 alt rows and at the same time, on the third row inc 2 sts around the 3 center sts (54 sts). To make the back of the shoe, mark row 11, then work 4 rows. Using a fine needle, pick up on the wrong side of the work each st from row 11 to work the other side of the shoe, knitting them together with the sts on the left-hand needle. On the next row, bind (cast) off 22 sts at each end. Make the sole with the 10 sts remaining, working a further 24 rows. Bind (cast) off.

Stitch the sole and sides together. Close the seam at the back with slip stitch. Hold the front of the upper to the sides with a few stitches. Use fine cord, carefully inserting it through the knitted stitches, to resemble laces, and fasten it with a neat bow.

Baby Bear

Back and front
The suit is worked in a single piece, beginning at the bottom of the left leg.

Using no. 3 (3¼mm) needles and Powder, cast on 34 sts. Work 4 rows in garter st. Change to no. 4 (3¾mm) needles and Diamond White, and work in st st, inc 2 sts at each end of the fifth row (38 sts). Leave these on a spare needle. Work the right leg in the same way and put all sts on a single needle (76 sts). Use pins or sewing thread to mark the 19th and 20th sts, the 38th and 39th sts and the 57th and 58th sts. Cont in st st. On the 7th, 13th and 19th rows dec 1 st at each end of the row and K2tog above each of the marked sts (52 sts). Row 25 (RS facing): K13, cast on 5 sts

(for the sleeve) and leave the remaining sts on a spare needle. Cont in st st on these 18 sts, dec 1 st at the right-hand side on the 1st, 7th and 13th rows. Shape the neck by binding (casting) off 4 sts on the 15th row. Cont to shape the neck by binding (casting) off 2 sts on the next row and 1 st on the next row (8 sts). Leave the sts on a spare needle.

Return to the 39 sts held and work as from row 25, but reversing all shaping, to make the left sleeve and shape the neck.

Return to the 26 sts held in the center. Cast on 5 sts at each end for the sleeves (36 sts). In the center of the 5th and 11th rows dec by 2 sts. On the 13th row shape the neck by binding (casting) off the center 8 sts. Work each side separately, shaping the neck by decreasing 2 sts on consecutive rows. Leave the remaining 8 sts for each shoulder on a spare needle.

Hood

Using no. 3 (3¼mm) needles and Powder, cast on 60 sts. Work 4 rows in garter st, working 6 dec across the last row (54 sts). Change to no. 4 (3¾mm) and Diamond White and cont in st st. When the work measures 1½in (4cm) from the beg, bind (cast) off 18 sts at each end. Cont in st st until the work measures 5½in (14cm) from the beg. Bind (cast) off.

Making up
Knit together the shoulder and top arm

seams on the inside. Make the cuffs. Using no. 3 (3¼mm) needles and Powder, pick up 28 sts around the bottom of each sleeve. Work 4 rows in garter st. Bind (cast) off. Join the underarm seams.

Make the neckband. Using no. 3 (3¼mm) needles and Powder, pick up 55 sts from around the neck. Work 4 rows in garter st. Bind (cast) off.

Make the bands down the front. Using no. 3 (3¼mm) needles and Powder, pick up 28 sts from one front opening and work 4 rows in garter st. Bind (cast) off. Repeat on the other side. Stitch the under leg seam, making sure that the front bands overlap each other. Close the seams on the hood and attach it to the neck, below the neckband.

Attach the Velcro strip down the front. Stitch on the buttons to decorate.

Teddy is waiting in the playroom for all his friends. He has got the yo-yo and dominoes from the boxes where they are kept so that they do not waste time looking for their favorite toys. He is wearing a special sweater, which his mother knitted for him for the last day of term.

Playing Games

Teddy

To fit a bear 13½in (34cm) tall

Wool
Wendy Courtelle (machine washable): 1 ball each of Light Brown (289), Champagne (184), Orange (128) and Saxe Blue (75)

Needles
1 pair of no. 2 (3mm) and 1 pair no. 3 (3¼mm)

Materials
6 cream-colored buttons, ¾in (15mm) across

Stitches
Rib: K1, P1 or K3, P3 (see pattern)
Striped pattern: work *5 rows Light Brown, 3 rows Champagne, 1 row Saxe Blue and 3 rows Orange*, repeating from * to *

Gauge (Tension)
Using no. 3 (3¼in) and measured over K3, P3 rib, 54 sts and 38 rows measure 4in (10cm) square.

Back

Using no. 3 (3¼mm) needles and Light Brown, cast on 75 sts and work in striped pattern and K3, P3 rib. When the work measures 1½in (4cm) from the beg, shape the arms by casting on 33 sts at each end (141 sts). Cont in K3, P3 rib until the work measures 4½in (11.5cm) from the beg. Bind (cast) off.

Front

Work as for the back, but bind (cast) off when the work measures 4¼in (11cm) from the beg.

Buttonband and buttonhole band

Using no. 2 (3mm) needles and Champagne, cast on 11 sts. Work 3½in (9cm) in K1, P1 rib. Bind (cast) off. Make another buttonband to match. Make a buttonhole band in the same way, but making 3 buttonholes, the first ¼in (5mm) from the beg and the others spaced 1½in (4cm) apart. Make the second buttonhole band in the same way.

Making up

Stitch the buttonbands to the back shoulders. Stitch the buttonhole bands to the front shoulders. Stitch on the buttons. Stitch the side and underarm seams.

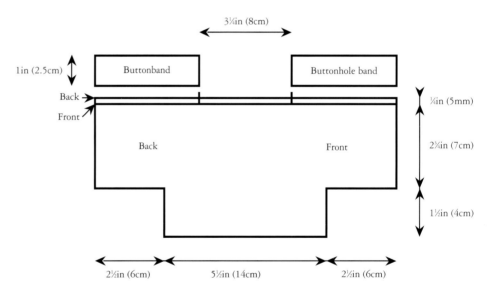

It is autumn and there is a distinct chill in the air and mists in the morning. Teddy has put on a warm cardigan and matching beret because he is going into the garden to pick some apples. His mother is going to make a delicious apple tart for supper, and while she waits for Teddy to come back with the apples, she is watching him through the kitchen window.

Teddy

To fit a bear 13½in (34cm) tall

Wool
Wendy Courtelle DK (machine washable): 1 ball each of Champagne (184), Forest (48) and Rust (274)

Needles
1 pair of no. 2 (3mm) needles

Materials
3 small metal buttons

Stitches
Rib: K1, P1
Stockinette (stocking) stitch (st st): knit 1 row, purl 1 row
Fair Isle (Jacquard): follow the chart opposite, using the stranding method (carrying the yarn not in use at the back of the work)

Gauge (Tension)
Using no. 2 (3mm) needles and measured over Fair Isle (Jacquard), 33 sts and 34 rows measure 4in (10cm) square.

Child

To fit a child 3/6 months

Wool
Wendy Courtelle DK (machine washable): 3 balls of Forest (48) and 2 balls each of Champagne (184) and Rust (274)

Needles
1 pair of no. 2 (3mm) needles

Materials
5 small metal buttons

Stitches
Rib: K1, P1
Stockinette (stocking) stitch (st st): knit 1 row, purl 1 row
Fair Isle (Jacquard): follow the chart opposite, using the stranding method (carrying the yarn not in use at the back of the work)

Gauge (Tension)
Using no. 2 (3mm) needles and measured over Fair Isle (Jacquard), 33 sts and 34 rows measure 4in (10cm) square.

Beret

To fit a bear 13½in (34cm) tall or a child 3 months old

Wool
Wendy Courtelle DK (machine washable): 1 ball each of Champagne (184), Forest (48) and Rust (274)

Needles
1 pair of no. 2 (3mm) needles and 1 pair of double-pointed no. 3 (3¼mm)

Materials
3 small metal buttons

Stitches
Rib: K1, P1
Stockinette (stocking) stitch (st st): knit 1 row, purl 1 row
Striped st st: see the pattern

Gauge (Tension)
Using no. 3 (3¼mm) needles and measured over stockinette (stocking) stitch, 26 sts and 35 rows measure 4in (10cm) square.

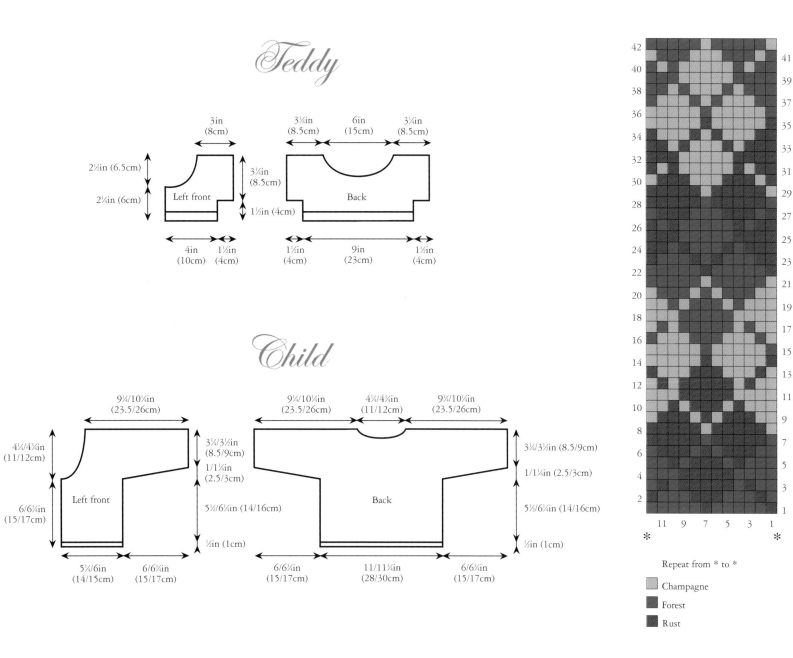

Teddy

3in (8cm)

2½in (6.5cm)

2¼in (6cm)

Left front

4in (10cm)   1½in (4cm)

3¼in (8.5cm)   6in (15cm)   3¼in (8.5cm)

3¼in (8.5cm)

Back

1½in (4cm)

1½in (4cm)   9in (23cm)   1½in (4cm)

Child

9¼/10¼in (23.5/26cm)

4¼/4¾in (11/12cm)

6/6¾in (15/17cm)

Left front

3¼/3½in (8.5/9cm)

1/1¼in (2.5/3cm)

5½/6¼in (14/16cm)

½in (1cm)

5½/6in (14/15cm)   6/6¾in (15/17cm)

9¼/10¼in (23.5/26cm)   4¼/4¾in (11/12cm)   9¼/10¼in (23.5/26cm)

Back

3¼/3½in (8.5/9cm)

1/1¼in (2.5/3cm)

5½/6¼in (14/16cm)

½in (1cm)

6/6¾in (15/17cm)   11/11¾in (28/30cm)   6/6¾in (15/17cm)

Repeat from * to *

Champagne
Forest
Rust

Teddy

Back and sleeves

Using no. 2 (3mm) needles and Forest, cast on 79 sts. Work in K1, P1 rib for ½in (1cm). Work in st st and begin to follow chart, starting with square 4. When the work measures 1½in (4cm) from the beg, shape the sleeves by casting on 12 sts at each end (103 sts). When the work measures 4¾in (10.5cm) from the beg, shape the neck by binding (casting) off the center 17 sts. Work each side separately. Cont to shape the neck by binding (casting) off 5 sts three times on alt rows (28 sts). When the work measures 4¾in (12.5cm) from the beg, bind (cast) off.

Left front and sleeve

Using no. 2 (3mm) needles and Forest, cast on 33 sts. Work in K1, P1 rib for ½in (1cm). Work in st st and begin to follow chart, starting with square 4. When the work measures 1½in (4cm) from the beg, shape the sleeve by casting on 12 sts (45 sts). When the work measures 2¼in (6cm) from the beg, shape the neck by binding (casting) off at the neck edge 1 st 12 times and, then, on alt rows, 1 st five times (28 sts). When the work measures 4¾in (12.5cm) from the beg, bind (cast) off.

Right front and sleeve

Work as for the left front, reversing all shaping.

Making up

Stitch the shoulder and upper arm seams. Make the cuffs. Using no. 2 (3mm) needles and Forest, pick up 61 sts from the bottom of the sleeve. Work in K1, P1 rib for ½in (1cm). Bind (cast) off. Repeat on the other sleeve.

Make the buttonband and neckband. Using no. 2 (3mm) needles and Forest, pick up 20 sts up the left front, 28 sts up the slope, 46 sts around the neck, 28 sts down the slope and 20 sts from the right front. Work in K1, P1 rib for ½in (1cm), working 3 buttonholes in one front band, with the first hole 3 sts from the bottom and the others 7 sts apart. Bind (cast) off. Stitch the side and underarm seams. Stitch on the buttons.

Child

Back and sleeves

Using no. 2 (3mm) needles and Forest, cast on 93/99 sts. Work in K1, P1 rib for ½in (1cm). Work in st st and begin to follow chart, starting with square 9/6. When the work measures 6/6¾in (15/17cm) from the beg, shape the sleeves by casting on at each end 12/11 sts twice/three times and 13/10 sts twice/twice on alt rows (193/205 sts). When the work measures 9¾/11in (25/28cm) from the beg, shape the neck by binding (casting) off the center 17/21 sts. Work each side separately. Cont to shape the neck by binding (casting) off 5 sts twice on alt rows (78/82 sts). When the work measures 10¼/11½in (26/29cm) from the beg, bind (cast) off.

Left front and sleeve

Using no. 2 (3mm) needles and Forest, cast on 46/49 sts. Work in K1, P1 rib for ½in (1cm). Work in st st and begin to follow chart, starting with square 9/6. When the work measures 6/6¾in (15/17cm) from the beg, shape the sleeve by casting on 12/11 sts twice/three times and 13/10 sts twice/twice on alt rows (96/102 sts). At the same time, shape the V-neck at the opposite side by decreasing on each row 1 st 12 times and, on alt rows, 1 st six/eight times (78/82 sts). When the work measures 10¼/11½in (26/29cm) from the beg, bind (cast) off.

Right front and sleeve

Work as for the left front, reversing all shaping.

Making up

Stitch the shoulder and upper arm seams. Make the cuffs. Using no. 2 (3mm) needles and Forest, pick up 61/65 sts from the bottom of the sleeve. Work in K1, P1 rib for ½in (1cm). Bind (cast) off. Repeat on the other sleeve.

Make the buttonband and neckband. Using no. 2 (3mm) needles and Forest, pick up 49/55 sts up the left front, 33/36 sts up the slope, 33/36 sts around the neck, 33/36 sts down the slope and 49/55 sts from the right front. Work in K1, P1 rib for ½in (1cm), working 5 buttonholes in one front band, with the first hole 3 sts from the bottom and the others 10/11 sts apart. Bind (cast) off. Stitch the side and underarm seams. Stitch on the buttons.

Beret

Using no. 2 (3mm) needles and Rust, cast on 138 sts. Work in K1, P1 rib for ¾in (2cm). Change to no. 3 (3¼mm) and cont working in striped st st, setting colors as follows: 8 rows Rust; 2 rows Champagne; 2 rows Rust; 7 rows Champagne; 5 rows Forest; 4 rows Rust; 2 rows Champagne; 2 rows Rust; 4 rows Champagne; 2 rows Forest; 2 rows Champagne; 4 rows Forest; 2 rows Rust; 2 rows Forest; 4 rows Rust; 2 rows Champagne; 1 row Rust; 2 rows Champagne; 1 row Forest; 1 row Champagne; 2 rows Forest; 1 row Rust; 1 row Forest; 2 rows Rust; 1 row Champagne; 1 row Rust; 2 rows Champagne. Finish by alternating 1 row Forest and 1 row Champagne. To avoid breaking and tying in colors, use double-pointed needles so that you can pick up colors as necessary at the end of the row.

Row 1: Sl1, *make a st, K17*, repeat from * to * seven times more, K1 into the back of the st (146 sts). On purl rows, purl the first st and slip the last st. Repeat the increases, positioning them above each other, seven times more on alt rows (202sts). Work 6 rows, then begin to dec. Next row: Sl1, *sl1, psso, work 23*, repeat from * to * eight times more, sl1. Repeat the decreases, positioning them above each other, seven times on alt rows, once after 4 rows, five times on alt rows, once after 4 rows, then on alt rows until only 10 sts remain. Pull the wool through the sts. Use the end of wool to join the seam. Make a pompom with all the colors of wool to decorate the top (see page 45).

Going Fishing

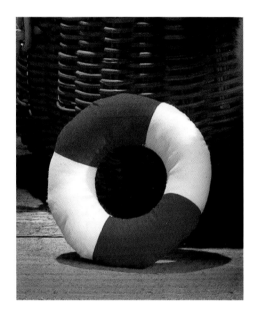

While he has been on holiday, Teddy has been fishing in the hope of catching some shrimps. He has been sitting on the end of the pier and has found the sea breeze rather chilly, so he has put on his warm sweater. He has not had much luck with the shrimps, but he is quite happy just watching the waves break on the shore.

Going Fishing

Teddy

To fit a bear 13½in (34cm) tall

Wool
Sunbeam St Ives 4-ply (machine washable): 1 ball each of Estuary (3096), Pheasant (3106), Navy (3110), Gunmetal (3062) and Heron (3105)

Needles
1 pair no. 2 (3mm) and 1 pair no. 3 (3¼mm)

Materials
1 strip of Velcro, 4in (10cm) long

Stitches
Rib: K2, P2
Stockinette (stocking) stitch (st st): knit 1 row, purl 1 row
Fair Isle (Jacquard): follow the chart opposite, using the stranding method (carrying the yarn not in use at the back of the work)

Gauge (Tension)
Using no. 3 (3¼mm) needles and measured over Fair Isle (Jacquard), 30 sts and 34 rows measure 4in (10cm) square.

Child

To fit a child 3/6 months

Wool
Sunbeam St Ives 4-ply (machine washable): 2 balls of Navy (3110) and 1 ball each of Estuary (3096), Pheasant (3106), Gunmetal (3062) and Heron (3105)

Needles
1 pair no. 2 (3mm) and 1 pair no. 3 (3¼mm)

Materials
6 small buttons

Stitches
Rib: K2, P2
Stockinette (stocking) stitch (st st): knit 1 row, purl 1 row
Fair Isle (Jacquard): follow the chart opposite, using the stranding method (carrying the yarn not in use at the back of the work)

Gauge (Tension)
Using no. 3 (3¼mm) needles and measured over Fair Isle (Jacquard), 30 sts and 34 rows measure 4in (10cm) square.

Teddy

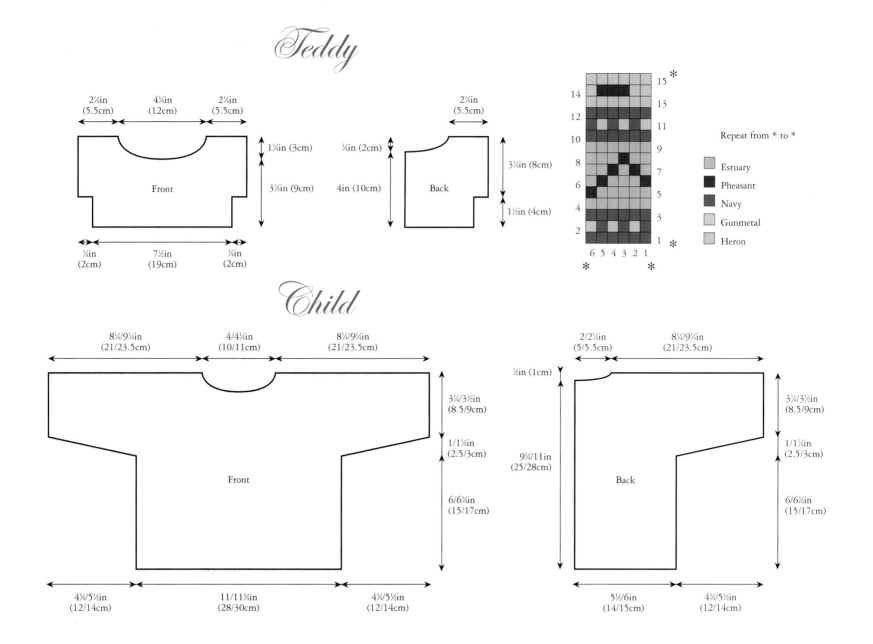

Front

2¼in (5.5cm) · 4¾in (12cm) · 2¼in (5.5cm)

1¼in (3cm)

3½in (9cm)

¾in (2cm) · 7½in (19cm) · ¾in (2cm)

Back

2¼in (5.5cm)

¾in (2cm)

3¼in (8cm)

4in (10cm)

1½in (4cm)

Repeat from * to *

- Estuary
- Pheasant
- Navy
- Gunmetal
- Heron

Child

Front

8¼/9¼in (21/23.5cm) · 4/4¼in (10/11cm) · 8¼/9¼in (21/23.5cm)

3¼/3½in (8.5/9cm)

1/1¼in (2.5/3cm)

6/6¾in (15/17cm)

4¾/5½in (12/14cm) · 11/11¾in (28/30cm) · 4¾/5½in (12/14cm)

Back

2/2¼in (5/5.5cm) · 8¼/9¼in (21/23.5cm)

½in (1cm)

9¾/11in (25/28cm)

3¼/3½in (8.5/9cm)

1/1¼in (2.5/3cm)

6/6¾in (15/17cm)

5½/6in (14/15cm) · 4¾/5½in (12/14cm)

Teddy

Front

Using no. 2 (3mm) needles and Navy, cast on 58 sts. Work in K2, P2 rib for 1½in (4cm), inc by 1 st in the center of the last row (59 sts). Change to no. 3 (3¼mm) needles and st st and begin to follow chart, starting with square 4 of the chart. On the third row, inc for the sleeves, casting on 6 sts at each end (71 sts). Cont in pattern as set until the work measures 3½in (9cm) from the beg. Bind (cast) off the center 9 sts for the neck opening and work each side separately. Cont in pattern, shape the neck by binding (casting) off 5 sts once, 4 sts once, 3 sts once and 1 st twice on alt rows (17 sts). Cont in pattern until the work measures 4¾in (12cm) from the beg. Bind (cast) off. Complete the other side to match, reversing all shaping.

Back

Using no. 2 (3mm) needles and Navy, cast on 30 sts. Work in K2, P2 rib for 1½in (4cm). Change to no. 3 (3¼mm) needles and begin to follow chart, starting with square 4 of the chart. On the third row, inc for the sleeves, casting on 6 sts at one end (36 sts). Cont in pattern as set until the work measures 4in (10cm) from the beg. Shape the neck by binding (casting) off 9 sts once and 5 sts twice on alt rows (17 sts). Cont in pattern until the work measures 4¾in (12cm) from the beg. Bind (cast) off. Work the other back to match, reversing all shaping.

Making up

Stitch the shoulder and upper arm seams. Make the cuffs. Using no. 2 (3mm) needles and Navy, pick up 58 sts from the bottom of a sleeve. Work in K2, P2 rib for 1½in (4cm). Bind (cast) off. Complete the other cuff to match.

Make the neckband. Using no. 2 (3mm) needles and Navy, pick up 86 sts around the neck. Work in K2, P2 rib for ¾in (2cm). Bind (cast) off.

Make the bands at the back. Using no. 2 (3mm) needles and Navy, pick up 36 sts from one side of the back. Work in K2, P2 rib

for ½in (1cm). Bind (cast) off. Work the second band to match.

Stitch the side and underarm seams. Attach the Velcro to the back opening.

Child

Front

Using no. 2 (3mm) needles and Navy, cast on 86/94 sts. Work in K2, P2 rib for 6/6½in (15/17cm), inc by 1 st in the center of the last row (87/95 sts). Change to no. 3 (3¼mm) needles and st st and begin to follow chart, starting with square 2/4 of the chart. On the third row, inc for the sleeves, casting on 4 sts nine times/9 sts twice and 8 sts three times at each end on alt rows (159/179 sts). Cont in pattern as set until the work measures 9/10¼in (23/26cm) from the beg. Bind (cast) off the center 17/21 sts for the neck opening and work each side separately. Cont in pattern, shape the neck by binding (casting) off 3/3 sts once, 2/2 sts once and 1/1 st twice on alt rows (64/72 sts). Cont in pattern until the work measures 10¼/11½in (26/29cm) from the beg. Bind (cast) off. Complete the other side, reversing all shaping.

Back

Using no. 2 (3mm) needles and Navy, cast on 42/46 sts. Work in K2, P2 rib for 6/6½in (15/17cm). Change to no. 3 (3¼mm) needles and begin to follow chart, starting with square 2/4 of the chart. On the third row, inc for the sleeves, casting on 9 sts four times/9 sts twice and 8 sts three times on alt rows (78/88 sts). Cont in pattern as set until the work measures 9¾/11in (25/28cm) from the beg. Shape the neck by binding (casting) off 7/8 sts twice on alt rows (64/72 sts). Cont in pattern until the work measures 10¼/11½in (26/29cm) from the beg. Bind (cast) off. Work the other back to match, reversing all shaping.

Making up

Stitch the shoulder and upper arm seams. Make the cuffs. Using no. 2 (3mm) needles and Navy, pick up 62/66 sts from the bottom of a sleeve. Work in K2, P2 rib for 2in (5cm). Bind (cast) off. Complete the other cuff to match.

Make the neckband. Using no. 2 (3mm) needles and Navy, pick up 86/90 sts around the neck. Work in K2, P2 rib for ¾in (2cm). Bind (cast) off.

Make the buttonband. Using no. 2 (3mm) needles and Navy, pick up 74/84 sts from one side of the back. Work in K2, P2 rib for ½in (1cm). Bind (cast) off. Work the buttonhole band to match, making buttonholes, the first 3 sts down from the top and the rest 12/14 sts apart.

Stitch the side and underarm seams. Stitch on the buttons.

Teddy is in the forest with his friend the squirrel, looking for mushrooms, chestnuts and hazelnuts, and they have managed to fill his basket with treasures, which mother will cook for them. They have promised to be home before it begins to get dark and before the squirrel eats all the nuts they have found.

In the Forest

Teddy

To fit a bear 13½in (34cm) tall

Wool
*Wendy Courtelle 4-ply (machine washable):
1 ball each of Tartan (2984), Oatmeal (81)
and Cherry Red (84)
Wendy Courtelle DK (machine washable):
odd length of Rust (274)*

Needles
*1 pair no. 2 (3mm), 1 pair no. 3 (3¼mm),
a spare needle and a darning needle*

Materials
1 strip of Velcro, 4in (10cm) long

Stitches
*Rib: K1, P1
Stockinette (stocking) stitch (st st): knit 1
row, purl 1 row
Fair Isle (Jacquard): follow Chart B, using
the stranding method (carrying the yarn not
in use at the back of the work)
Swiss darning: on the finished sweater cover
individual knitted stitches with V-shaped
stitches worked in wool*

Gauge (Tension)
*Using no. 3 (3¼mm) needles and measured
over stockinette (stocking) stitch, 29 sts and
36 rows measure 4in (10cm) square.*

Child

To fit a child 3/6 months

Wool
*Wendy Courtelle 4-ply (machine washable):
2 balls of Oatmeal (81); 1 ball each of
Tartan (2984) and Cherry Red (84)
Wendy Courtelle DK (machine washable):
odd length of Rust (274)*

Needles
*1 pair no. 2 (3mm), 1 pair no. 3 (3¼mm),
a spare needle and a darning needle*

Materials
6 small buttons

Stitches
*Rib: K1, P1
Stockinette (stocking) stitch (st st): knit 1
row, purl 1 row
Fair Isle (Jacquard): follow Chart B, using
the stranding method (carrying the yarn not
in use at the back of the work)
Swiss darning: on the finished sweater cover
individual knitted stitches with V-shaped
stitches worked in wool*

Gauge (Tension)
*Using no. 3 (3¼mm) needles and measured
over stockinette (stocking) stitch, 29 sts and
36 rows measure 4in (10cm) square.*

Teddy

Child

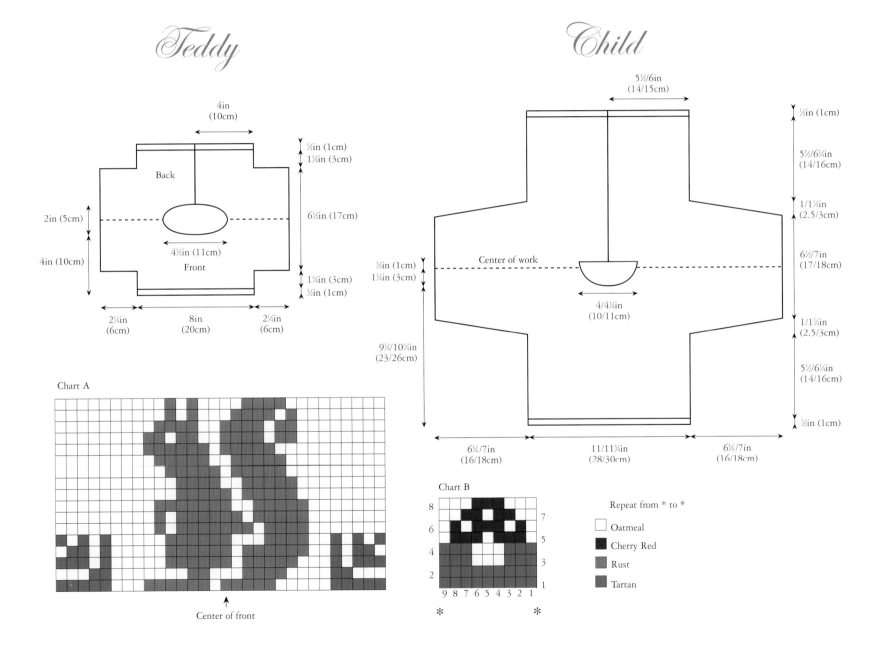

4in
(10cm)

Back

½in (1cm)
1¼in (3cm)

2in (5cm)

6½in (17cm)

4in (10cm)

4½in (11cm)

Front

1¼in (3cm)
½in (1cm)

2¼in
(6cm)

8in
(20cm)

2¼in
(6cm)

5½/6in
(14/15cm)

½in (1cm)

5½/6¼in
(14/16cm)

1/1¼in
(2.5/3cm)

6½/7in
(17/18cm)

Center of work

4/4¼in
(10/11cm)

1/1¼in
(2.5/3cm)

½in (1cm)
1¼in (3cm)

5½/6¼in
(14/16cm)

9¼/10¼in
(23/26cm)

½in (1cm)

6¼/7in
(16/18cm)

11/11¾in
(28/30cm)

6¼/7in
(16/18cm)

Chart A

Center of front

Chart B

8

6

4

2

7

5

3

1

9 8 7 6 5 4 3 2 1

*   *

Repeat from * to *

☐ Oatmeal

■ Cherry Red

■ Rust

■ Tartan

In the Forest

Teddy

The sweater is worked in a single piece, starting with the bottom front.

Using no. 2 (3mm) needles and Tartan, cast on 63 sts. Work in K1, P1 rib for ½in (1cm). Change to no. 3 (3¼mm) needles and st st, and beg to follow Chart B for 8 rows (starting on square 1), stranding the wool not in use by carrying it loosely at the back of the work. Cont in st st in Oatmeal only. When the work measures 1½in (4cm) from the beg, dec 1 st at each end of the next row. At each end of the following row cast on 10 sts for the sleeves (81 sts). Cont in st st. When the work measures 4in (10cm) from the beg, shape the neck by binding (casting) off the center 11 sts. Work each side separately. Cont to shape the neck by binding (casting) off 3 sts once, 2 sts twice and 1 st four times on alt rows (24 sts). Cont in st st for 4 rows and then shape the back of the neck, inc by 2 sts once, 4 sts twice and 6 sts once on alt rows (40 sts). Cont until the work measures 8½in (21cm) from the beg. Bind (cast) off 10 sts to complete the sleeve. Next row: inc 1 st (31 sts). Cont in st st until the work measures 8¾in (22cm) from the beg, work 8 rows from Chart B, starting at the top. Change to no. 2 (3mm) needles and work in K1, P1 rib for ½in (1cm). Bind (cast) off. Complete the other sleeve and back to match, reversing all shaping.

Making up

Using Rust and scraps of Tartan, follow Chart A to embroider the squirrel and leaves on the center of the front, leaving 2 clear rows above the mushrooms.

Make the cuffs. Using no. 2 (3mm) needles and Oatmeal, pick up 58 sts from the end of the sleeves. Work in K1, P1 rib for ½in (1cm) and bind (cast) off. Repeat on the other sleeve.

Make the neckband. Using no. 2 (3mm) needles and Oatmeal, pick up 87 sts around the neck. Work in K1, P1 rib for ½in (1cm) and bind (cast) off.

Make the bands up the back. Using no. 2 (3mm) needles and Oatmeal, pick up 39 sts up one side. Work in K1, P1 rib for ½in (1cm) and bind (cast) off. Repeat on the other side.

Stitch the side and underarm seams. Attach the Velcro to the back bands.

Child

The sweater is worked in a single piece, starting with the bottom front.

Using no. 2 (3mm) needles and Tartan, cast on 81/87 sts. Work in K1, P1 rib for ½in (1cm). Change to no. 3 (3¼mm) needles and st st, and beg to follow Chart B for 8 rows (starting on square 1/7), stranding the wool not in use by carrying it loosely at the back of the work. Cont in st st in Oatmeal only. When the work measures 6/6¾in (15/17cm) from the beg, make the sleeves, casting on 11 sts twice and 12 sts twice/11 sts twice and 10 sts three times at each end of alt rows (173/191 sts). Cont in st st. When the work measures 9/10¼in (23/26cm) from the beg, shape the neck by binding (casting) off the center 17/21 sts. Work each side separately. Cont to shape the neck by binding (casting) off 3/3 sts once, 2/2 sts once and 1/1 st once on alt rows (72/79 sts). Cont in st st until the work measures 10½/11¾in (27/30cm) from the beg, and then shape the back of the neck, inc by 14/16 sts once (86/95 sts). Cont until the work measures 13½/15in (34.5/38cm) from the beg. Complete the sleeve by binding (casting) off 11 sts twice and 12 sts twice/11 sts twice and 10 sts three times on alt rows (40/43 sts). Cont in st st until the work measures 19¼/21½in (49/55cm) from the beg, work 8 rows from Chart B, starting at the top and matching the pattern. Change to no. 2 (3mm) needles and work in K1, P1 rib for ½in (1cm). Bind (cast) off. Complete the other sleeve and back to match, reversing all shaping.

Making up

Using Rust and scraps of Tartan, follow Chart A to embroider the squirrel and leaves on the center of the front, leaving 2 clear rows above the mushrooms.

Make the cuffs. Using no. 2 (3mm) needles and Oatmeal, pick up 59/65 sts from the end of the sleeves. Work in K1, P1 rib for ½in (1cm) and bind (cast) off. Repeat on the other sleeve.

Make the neckband. Using no. 2 (3mm) needles and Oatmeal, pick up 87/93 sts around the neck. Work in K1, P1 rib for ½in (1cm) and bind (cast) off.

Make the buttonband up the back. Using no. 2 (3mm) needles and Oatmeal, pick up 77/87 sts up one side. Work in K1, P1 rib for ½in (1cm) and bind (cast) off. Make a buttonhole band in the same way, making 6 buttonholes, the first 3 sts down from the top, the others evenly spaced 13/15 sts apart.

Stitch the side and underarm seams. Stitch on the buttons to match the holes.

Teddy loves playing soccer, and his
mother has knitted him a sweater in
his favorite team's colors, decorating it
with little buttons that look like soccer
balls. One day, he dreams, he will play
for his country, but in the meantime he
enjoys playing with his friends in the
school team.

Playing Soccer

Teddy

To fit a bear 13½in (34cm) tall

Wool
Wendy Courtelle 4-ply (machine washable):
1 ball each of White (70) and Raven (89)

Needles
1 pair no. 2 (3mm), 1 pair no. 3 (3¼mm)
and a darning needle

Materials
6 buttons resembling soccer balls
1 strip of Velcro, 4½in (11cm) long

Stitches
Rib: K1, P1
Stockinette (stocking) stitch (st st): knit 1
row, purl 1 row
Striped st st: work 2 rows in White, 2 rows
in Raven
Swiss darning: on the finished sweater cover
individual knitted stitches with V-shaped
stitches worked in Raven following the chart
opposite

Gauge (Tension)
Using no. 3 (3¼mm) needles and measured
over stockinette (stocking) stitch, 28 stitches
and 37 rows measure 4in (10cm) square.

Front

Using no. 2 (3mm) and Raven, cast on 57 sts. Work in K1, P1 rib for ½in (1cm). Change to no. 3 (3¼mm) needles and st st. (You will find it easier to use two balls of Raven.) Row 1: K28 in Raven, K1 in White, K28 in Raven. Row 2: P27 in Raven, P3 in White, P27 in Raven. Cont in pattern as set until all 57 sts are in White. Cont in st st until work measures 3¼in (9cm) from the beg. Shape the neck by binding (casting) off the center 9 sts. Work each side separately, dec on alt row by 3 sts once, 2 sts three times and 1 st twice (13 sts). Cont until work measures 4½in (12cm) from the beg. Bind (cast) off. Work the other shoulder, reversing all shaping.

Back

Using no. 2 (3mm) and Raven, cast on 28 sts. Work in K1, P1 rib for ½in (1cm). Change to no. 3 (3¼mm) needles and st st. Row 1: K27 in Raven, K1 in White. Row 2: P2 in White, P26 in Raven. Cont in pattern as set until all 28 sts are in White. When the work measures 4in (10cm) from the beg, shape the neck by binding (casting) off 10 sts once, 2 sts twice and 1 st once on alt rows (13 sts). Cont until the work measures 4½in (12cm) from the beg. Bind (cast) off. Work the other back to match, reversing all shaping.

Sleeves

Join the shoulder seams. Using no. 3 (3¼mm) needles and White, pick up 22 sts over the 3in (8cm) of each shoulder shaping (44 sts). Work in striped st st until the sleeve is 2¾in (7cm) long. Change to no. 2 (3mm) needles and Raven and work in K1, P1 rib for ½in (1cm). Bind (cast) off. Work the other sleeve to match.

Making up

Using the chart as a guide and Raven, embroider the diamond pattern across the front. Stitch on the buttons. Make the neckband. Using no. 2 (3mm) needles and White, pick up 81 sts and work in K1, P1 rib for ½in (1cm). Bind (cast) off. Make the bands down the back. Using no. 2 (3mm) needles and matching the Raven and White pattern, pick up 41 sts down one back opening. Work in K1, P1 rib for ½in (1cm). Bind (cast) off. Repeat on the other side. Join the side and underarm seams. Attach the Velcro to the back bands.

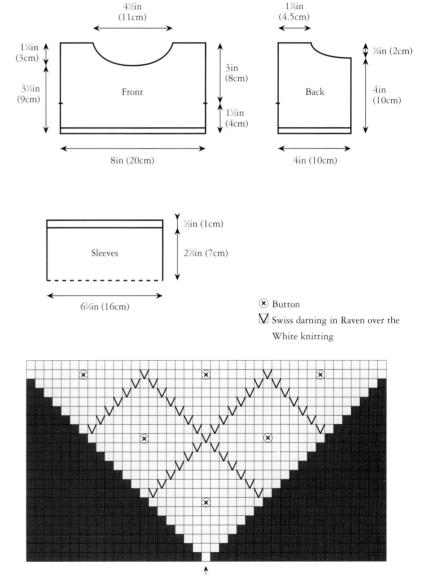

4½in (11cm)

1¼in (3cm)

3¼in (9cm)

3in (8cm)

1½in (4cm)

Front

8in (20cm)

1¾in (4.5cm)

¾in (2cm)

4in (10cm)

Back

4in (10cm)

½in (1cm)

2¾in (7cm)

Sleeves

6¼in (16cm)

⊗ Button

☑ Swiss darning in Raven over the White knitting

↑ Center of front

Teddy is going to have a tea party for his friends, and he hopes that they will admire his smart new sweater, which his mother knitted for him to wear at his party. He is going to give his friends some of their favorite biscuits and some home-made jam. It is a special occasion, and they are going to use the best tea set.

Tea Time

Teddy

To fit a bear 13½in (34cm) tall

Wool
Robin Columbine 4-ply (machine washable):
2 balls of Signal Red (6823)

Needles
1 pair no. 2 (3mm), 1 pair no. 3 (3¼mm),
a cable needle and a spare needle

Materials
1 strip of Velcro, 3½in (9cm) long

Stitches
Stockinette (stocking) stitch (st st): knit 1
row, purl 1 row
Garter stitch: knit every row
Cable: repeat the 9 sts and 8 rows of the
chart

Gauge (Tension)
Using no. 3 (3¼mm) needles and measured
over cable pattern, 36 sts and 38 rows
measure 4in (10cm) square.

Child

To fit a child 3/6 months

Wool
Robin Columbine 4-ply (machine washable):
3/4 balls of Signal Red (6823)

Needles
1 pair no. 2 (3mm), 1 pair no. 3 (3¼mm),
a cable needle and a spare needle

Materials
6 small buttons

Stitches
Stockinette (stocking) stitch (st st): knit 1
row, purl 1 row
Garter stitch: knit every row
Cable: repeat the 9 sts and 8 rows of the
chart

Gauge (Tension)
Using no. 3 (3¼mm) needles and measured
over cable pattern, 36 sts and 38 rows
measure 4in (10cm) square.

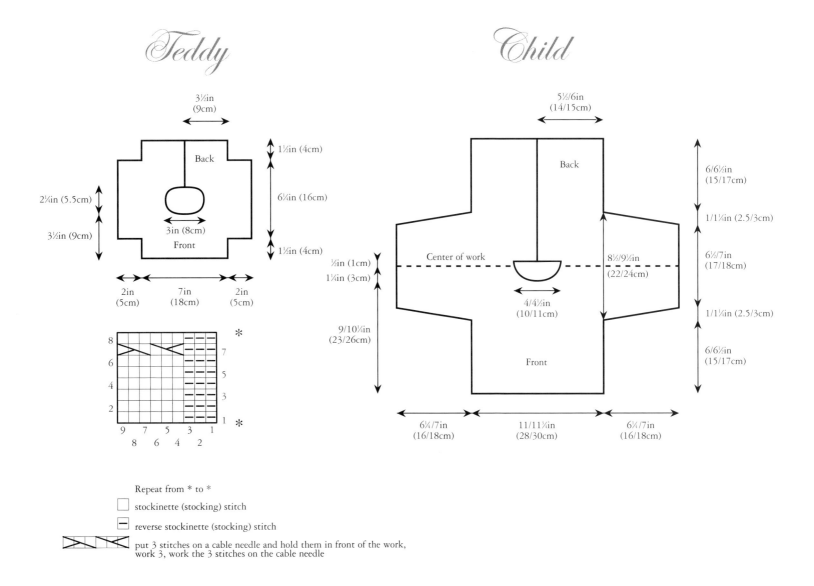

Teddy

3½in
(9cm)

1½in (4cm)

Back

2⅛in (5.5cm)

6¼in (16cm)

3½in (9cm)

3in (8cm)

Front

1½in (4cm)

2in
(5cm)

7in
(18cm)

2in
(5cm)

8 | | | | | ✱
7
6
5
4
3
2
1 | | | | | ✱
9 7 5 3 1
8 6 4 2

Child

5½/6in
(14/15cm)

Back

6/6½in
(15/17cm)

1/1⅛in (2.5/3cm)

Center of work

8½/9½in
(22/24cm)

6½/7in
(17/18cm)

½in (1cm)

1⅛in (3cm)

4/4½in
(10/11cm)

1/1⅛in (2.5/3cm)

9/10¼in
(23/26cm)

Front

6/6½in
(15/17cm)

6¼/7in
(16/18cm)

11/11¾in
(28/30cm)

6¼/7in
(16/18cm)

Repeat from * to *

☐ stockinette (stocking) stitch

⊟ reverse stockinette (stocking) stitch

put 3 stitches on a cable needle and hold them in front of the work,
work 3, work the 3 stitches on the cable needle

Tea Time

Teddy

The sweater is knitted as a single piece, starting at the bottom of the front.

Using no. 2 (3mm) needles, cast on 59 sts. Work 6 rows in st st, inc by 7 sts across the last row (66 sts). This will form the rolled hem. Change to no. 3 (3¼mm) needles and cont in cable pattern (see the chart). When the work measures 1½in (4cm) from the beg of the cable pattern, shape the sleeves by casting on 18 sts at each end (102 sts). Cont in cable pattern. When the work measures 3½in (9cm) from the beg of the cable pattern, shape the neck by binding (casting) off the center 10 sts. Working on each side separately, cont to shape the neck by binding (casting) off 4 sts once, 3 sts once and 2 sts once on alt rows (37 sts). Cont in cable pattern for 16 rows, then shape the back of the neck by casting on 6 sts twice on alt rows (49 sts). When the sleeve measures 6¼in (16cm), bind (cast) off 18 sts (31 sts). Cont in pattern to complete the left back. When the work measures 9¼in (24cm) from the beg of the cable pattern, change to no. 2 (3mm) needles and work 6 rows in st st, dec the first row by 1 st. Bind (cast) off loosely. Complete the other side to match, reversing all shaping.

Making up

Make the neckband. Using no. 2 (3mm) needles, pick up 76 sts from around the neck. Work 6 rows in st st and bind (cast) off. Allow the edging to roll over.

Make the bands down the back opening. Using no. 2 (3mm) needles, pick up 30 sts from one side of the back (do not pick up sts from the neckband or rolled hem) and work 6 rows in garter st. Bind (cast) off. Repeat on the other side.

Make the cuffs. Using no. 2 (3mm) needles, pick up 48 sts from the bottom of one sleeve and work 6 rows in st st. Repeat on the other sleeve.

Stitch the side and underarm seams. Attach the Velcro strip to the back opening.

Child

The sweater is knitted as a single piece, starting at the bottom of the front.

Using no. 2 (3mm) needles, cast on 91/99 sts. Work 6 rows in st st, inc by 11/12 sts across the last row (102/111 sts). This will form the rolled hem. Change to no. 3 (3¼mm) needles and cont in cable pattern (see the chart). When the work measures 6/6½in (15/17cm) from the beg of the cable pattern, shape the sleeves by casting on 12 sts twice and 11 sts three times/11 sts three times and 10 sts three times at each end on alt rows (216/237 sts). Cont in cable pattern. When the work measures 9/10¼in (23/26cm) from the beg of the cable pattern, shape the neck by binding (casting) off the center 20/23 sts. Working on each side separately, cont to shape the neck by binding (casting) off 3/3 sts once, 2/2 sts once and 1/1 st three times on alt rows (90/99 sts). Cont in cable pattern. When the work measures 10¾/12in (27/30cm) from the beg of the cable pattern shape the back of the neck by casting on 19/21 sts (109/120 sts). When the sleeve measures 7/7½in (18/19cm), bind (cast) off 12 sts twice and 11 sts three times/11 sts three times and 10 sts three times (52/57 sts). Cont in pattern to complete the left back. When the work measures 20½/22½in (52/58cm) from the beg of the cable pattern, change to no. 2 (3mm) needles and work 6 rows in st st, dec the first row by 1 st. Bind (cast) off loosely. Complete the other side to match, reversing all shaping.

Making up

Make the neckband. Using no. 2 (3mm) needles, pick up 76/82 sts from around the neck. Work 6 rows in st st and bind (cast) off. Allow the edging to roll over.

Make the buttonband down the back opening. Using no. 2 (3mm) needles, pick up 73/79 sts from one side of the back (do not pick up sts from the neckband or rolled hem) and work 6 rows in garter st. Bind (cast) off. Make the buttonhole band on the other side in the same way, but work 6 buttonholes, the first 3 sts from the neckband, the others spaced 12/13sts apart.

Make the cuffs. Using no. 2 (3mm) needles, pick up 50/56 sts from the bottom of one sleeve and work 6 rows in st st. Repeat on the other sleeve.

Stitch the side and underarm seams. Stitch on the buttons on the buttonband, positioning them to match the buttonholes.

It is time for bed, and Baby Bear has got
a new sleeping suit, which will keep him
snug and warm all night long. He can
play with his toys for a while before he
has to go to bed, but he will have to put
away his blocks before he gets into bed.
Mother Bear has knitted a bed jacket for
herself in matching colors.

Bed Time

Mother Bear

To fit a bear 13½in (34cm) tall

Wool
*Wendy Bambine 4-ply (machine washable):
1 ball each of Sunrise (1022) and Lilac
(1025)*

Needles
*1 pair no. 2 (3mm), 1 pair no. 3 (3¼mm)
and spare needles*

Materials
*1 small mother-of-pearl button
1 small snap (press-stud) or small piece of
Velcro*

Stitches
*Garter stitch: knit every row
Stockinette (stocking) stitch (st st): knit 1
row, purl 1 row
Pattern: *3 rows st st*, purl 1 row, rep from
* to *, knit 1 row*

Gauge (Tension)
*Using no. 3 (3¼mm) needles and measured
over stockinette (stocking) stitch, 26 stitches
and 31 rows measures 4in (10cm) square.*

Baby Bear

To fit a bear 9½in (24cm) tall

Wool
*Wendy Bambine 4-ply (machine washable):
1 ball each of Sunrise (1022) and Lilac
(1025)*

Needles
*1 pair no. 00 (2mm) needles, 1 pair no. 2
(3mm), 1 pair no. 3 (3¼mm) and spare
needles*

Materials
2 small mother-of-pearl buttons

Stitches
*Garter stitch: knit every row
Stockinette (stocking) stitch (st st): knit 1
row, purl 1 row
Pattern: beg with a knit row, work *three
rows st st*, knit 1 row; beg with a purl row
rep from * to *, purl 1 row*

Gauge (Tension)
*Using no. 3 (3¼mm) needles and measured
over stockinette (stocking) stitch, 26 stitches
and 31 rows measures 4in (10cm) square.*

Mother Bear

Baby Bear

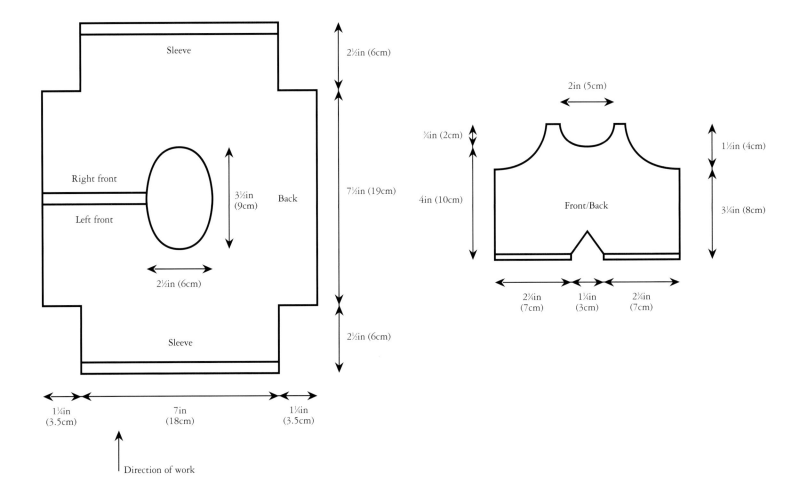

Mother Bear diagram labels: Sleeve, Right front, Left front, Back, Sleeve, 2½in (6cm), 7½in (19cm), 2½in (6cm), 3½in (9cm), 2½in (6cm), 1¼in (3.5cm), 7in (18cm), 1¼in (3.5cm), Direction of work

Baby Bear diagram labels: 2in (5cm), ¾in (2cm), 4in (10cm), Front/Back, 1½in (4cm), 3¼in (8cm), 2¾in (7cm), 1¼in (3cm), 2¾in (7cm)

Mother Bear

The jacket is knitted in a single piece, beg with the left sleeve.

Using no. 2 (3mm) needles and Sunrise, cast on 48 sts. Work 6 rows in garter st. Change to no. 3 (3¼mm) needles and Lilac, cont in pattern until the work measures 2½in (6cm) from the beg. To make the front and back, cast on 9 sts at each end of the next row (66 sts). Cont in pattern. When the work measures 4½in (11cm) from the beg, bind (cast) off the center 10 sts. Cont to work on the 28 sts on the left, putting the other sts on a spare needle. Work 2 rows then shape the neck at the left front by dec 3 sts once (25 sts). When the work measures 6¼in (15.5cm) from the beg, change to no. 2 (3mm) needles and Sunrise and work 6 rows in garter st. Bind (cast) off.

Work the right front. Using no. 2 (3mm) needles and Sunrise, cast on 25 sts and work 6 rows in garter st. Change to no. 3 (3¼mm) needles and Lilac, cont in pattern to shape the neck as for the left front, reversing all shaping. Put the sts on a spare needle.

Return to the sts held for the back and, keeping in pattern, work the neck opening to match the left side. Cont until the work measures 6¼in (15.5cm) from the beg, then work the neck opening to match the right front, finishing by binding (casting) off 10 sts. Pick up the sts held for the right front and, keeping in pattern, work the right arm to match the left.

Making up
Make the neckband. Using no. 2 (3mm) needles and Sunrise, pick up 110 sts from around the neck. Work 6 rows in garter st, making an extra st on alt rows twice at the corners. Bind (cast) off. Stitch the sides and underarm seams. Make an edging for the bottom of the jacket. Using no. 2 (3mm) needles and Sunrise, pick up 125 sts from around the bottom of the jacket and work 6 rows in garter st. Bind (cast) off. Stitch the snap (press-stud) to the top of the jacket. Stitch the button on top of the snap (press-stud).

Baby Bear

The front and back of the sleep suit are knitted as a single piece, beg at the bottom back of the left leg.

Using no. 2 (3mm) needles and Lilac, cast on 18 sts. Work 4 rows in garter st. Change to no. 3 (3¼mm) needles and Sunrise, cont in pattern, inc by 1 st at the right edge on alt rows four times. Leave the 22 sts on a spare needle. Work the right leg in the same way, reversing the shaping. Put both legs on a single needle (44 sts). Cont in pattern until the work measures 3¼in (8cm) from the beg, then shape the armholes, binding (casting) off 3 sts once, 2 sts twice and 1 st five times at both ends of alt rows. At the same time, when the work measures 4in (10cm) from the beg, bind (cast) off the center 8 sts and work each side separately, shaping the neck opening by dec 2 sts once and 1 st once on alt rows (3 sts). Bind (cast) off. Work the other side to match.

Making up

Make the front neckband. Using no. 00 (2mm) needles and Lilac, pick up 20 sts from each armhole shaping, 3 sts from the top of each strap and 20 sts around the neck. Work 4 rows in garter st, making 2 sts above each strap on the second row. Bind (cast) off.

Make the back neckband and straps. Using no. 00 (2mm) needles and Lilac, cast on 30 sts, then pick up 20 sts from an armhole shaping. Work 4 rows in garter st and bind (cast) off. Repeat at the other side. To complete the straps and the back neckband, using no. 00 (2mm) needles and Lilac, pick up 30 sts from each strap and 20 sts from the back neck. Work 4 rows in garter st and bind (cast) off. Make a buttonhole in one end of each strap by K2tog twice and, on the next row, making 1 st twice at the same point. Stitch the side and under-leg seams. Stitch a button on each front strap.

Techniques

Abbreviations

alt	alternate
beg	begin/beginning
cont	continue
dec	decrease
inc	increase
K	knit
K2tog	knit 2 sts together
P	purl
psso	pass slipped stitch over
rep	repeat
RS	right side
sl	slip
st/sts	stitch/stitches
st st	stockinette (stocking) stitch
tog	together
WS	wrong side

Gauge (Tension)

Check the gauge (tension) of your knitting before you begin. Because many of the patterns in this book are for small items, you will probably want to use odd balls of wool you already have, so work a piece 4in (10cm) square to check that your wool will knit up as the instructions. If your gauge (tension) square is larger than suggested, use smaller needles; if it is smaller, use larger needles.

Casting on with two needles

Make a slip loop and put it on the left-hand needle. Put the right-hand needle into the loop (1) and wind the yarn around it (2). Draw the yarn through the loop on the left-hand needle with the right-hand needle (3) and transfer the loop to the left-hand needle. Put the right-hand needle between the last two stitches on the left-hand needle (4) and wind the yarn around the needle as before.

(1)

(2)

(3)

(4)

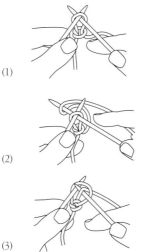

Casting on with the thumb

Make a slip loop, leaving an end of yarn about a yard (metre) long. Put the loop on a needle. Draw up both ends of the yarn to tighten the loop. Take the needle in your right hand and, with the yarn end in your left hand and the main yarn in your right hand (1), wind the yarn around your left hand in a X-shape and put the needle through the loop (2). Wind the main yarn around the needle and draw this loop through (3). Leave this stitch on the needle (4) and repeat.

(1)

(2)

(3)

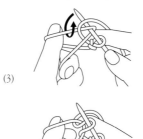

(4)

Knit stitches

With the needle holding the cast-on stitches in your left hand and the yarn at the back of the work, put the right-hand needle through the front of the first stitch to the back (1). Wind the yarn around the right-hand needle (2) and pull the new loop through the old loop (3) and onto the right-hand needle. Slip the old stitch off the left-hand needle.

(1)

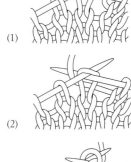

(2)

(3)

Purl stitches

With the needle holding the cast-on stitches in your left hand and the yarn at the front of the work, put the right-hand needle through the front of the first stitch and to the front of the work (1). Wind the yarn around the right-hand needle from above (2) and pull the new loop through the old loop and onto the right-hand needle (3). Slip the old stitch off the left-hand needle.

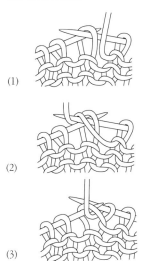

(1)

(2)

(3)

Picking up a dropped stitch with a crochet hook

On a knit row, with RS facing, insert the crochet hook from the front into the dropped stitch. Put the hook under the loop above the stitch and pull it through the stitch. Continue in this way until the stitch is level with the rest of the work. On a purl row, with WS facing, insert the crochet hook between the bottom and second loops lying above the dropped stitch, then into the stitch from back to front. Draw the yarn through the stitch. Put the new stitch on a spare needle and insert the hook between the next two threads above. Pick up the stitch from the needle and draw the yarn through.

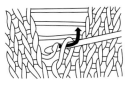

Wendy Wool Distributors

USA
Berroco Inc
14 Elmdale Road
Uxbridge, MA 01569
tel: 508 278 2527
fax: 508 278 2461

UK
Thomas B. Ramsden & Co.
(Bradford) Ltd
Netherfield Road
Guiseley
West Yorkshire LS20 9PD
tel: 01943 872264
fax: 01943 878689

Australia
TCW Pty Ltd
2/707 Forest Road
Peakhurst
New South Wales 2210
tel: 02 9584 8111
fax: 02 9584 8339

New Zealand
Wentworth Distributors
15 Church Street
Onehunga
Auckland
tel and fax: 09 634 0601

South Africa
Aladdin's Cave
tel: 011 975 2116
fax: 011 394 3036